Buck Jones

Copyright 2014

ISBN: 978 - 1 - 502 - 39857 - 4

A Buck's Worth
190 E. Stacy Rd #306-273
Allen, Tx 75002

PREFACE

I was living in the Chicago area at the time. On my sixteenth birthday I went down to the local supermarket and applied to be a bag boy. They didn't have any openings, but they kept my application and said they'd contact me if anything came up. So back home I went ... disappointed and discouraged.

To my surprise, two days later they called and asked if I'd be interested in working in the store's delicatessen. I didn't know what a delicatessen was but the job paid 12¢ more an hour than the bag boy job so I immediately said "yes." The next afternoon, nervous and scared, I walked into my local Dominick's Finer Foods for my first real job, and my life was never the same again.

Eighteen years and numerous job-titles later, I was a corporate vice president for one of the larger supermarket companies in America. In many ways I was amazed at how quickly it all happened and I learned a lot during those eighteen years. There were many good times and personal triumphs, as well as plenty of rough times, disappointments and failures. But more than that, there were so many things, especially in basic leadership and management areas, which I didn't learn until much later in my career. As I think back, I wish I'd known these basic concepts as I advanced through my retail experiences. I firmly believe I could have accomplished so much more and helped my employees and companies be even more successful. Of course in retail, that's not how it normally works.

In retail, leadership or management training is usually only conducted at the company executive level ... and the truth is, up to this time, that probably made the most sense. First, these programs are usually extremely expensive ... this causes costs to sky-rocket if we attempt to implement a program across hundreds of store-level managers. Second, it's extremely difficult time-wise to bring these managers together on any consistent basis to attend these kinds of training sessions.

But here's the problem ... in the retail environment, the two positions that have the greatest impact on an operation's success or failure are the department manager and the store manager. This has been proven to me over and over ... while personally holding these positions, and then during the last two decades while working with so many different retail companies. These managers are responsible for hiring, training and overseeing their work force, ... these managers are responsible for making sure the operational and merchandising programs are effectively executed ... and these managers are responsible for ensuring the company's customer service standards are met.

Make no mistake, no matter what retail industry (convenience store, fast-food, supermarket, restaurant, shoe stores, etc.), these managers are in the key positions. And that's why, not only can they personally benefit the most from this type of training, but they also offer the greatest potential return because they can immediately use it to effect their sales and profits.

That's why I chose to write this book ... and that's why we developed our "Think About It" video e-mail series. Today, it's a myth that store-level leadership and managerial training has to be expensive or time-consuming. That's just not the case. By using today's technology, material can be sent directly to each participant in a high-impact, cost-effective, timely and on-going fashion. Today, we can target managers with the specific information we want them to grasp with a program that is on-going so managers are continuously learning and growing.

So No! This is not just another leadership or management training book spouting one platitude after another in some endless unrelated format. Instead, this book is written for retailers, by a retailer, discussing what it takes to succeed while working in a retail store environment. To begin this process, I've selected topics for this book and the initial video e-mail series, which would have benefited me the most. These short singularly-focused clips address these issues in a story-format designed to help managers be more successful. In truth, only by helping managers be better and more successful, will their stores be better and more successful, which in turn makes their company better and more successful. Contrary to opinion, I've always found that's the way it works at retail ... from the stores UP, not the other way around!

As you browse through the book, you'll notice the chapters can be read and reviewed in short 15-minute periods. Hence the title, *"Success At Retail, One 15-Minute Break At A Time."* Managers can keep the book at work and review chapters while on a break. They can proceed at their own pace.

They'll also find a "Punch-In Ideas" section at the beginning of each chapter. Here I've included a few of my own thoughts managers might want to consider before "punching in" to read the chapter. Hopefully, these thoughts will set the stage for their reading.

At the end of the chapter, I've included a "Punch-Out Thoughts" section in conjunction with a "Notes" area. To maximize the chapter's effectiveness, as managers punch out, they should take a little time to read, think about how these points can best serve them and list out a few ideas of their own.

So as we begin, I hope you'll enjoy reading the material as much as I've enjoyed writing it ... but even more than that, as a retailer, I'm optimistic you'll find this information thoughtful, relevant and helpful in your own personal retail journey. Let me know what you think.

Buck Jones

A Buck's Worth
(214) 383-3442
buck@jonessco.com

Questions I Wish I'd Asked As A Retail Manager

A Buck's Worth
190 Stacy #306-273
Allen, Tx 75002
(214) 383-3442
www.abucksworth.com

A Buck's Worth

7	Now I'm A Manager, What Things Should I Do Differently?
15	What Can I Do To Help Me Learn, Advance And Grow?
22	Am I Paying You Right Now?
31	What Is Your Main Job Tonight?
37	Do You Understand Why?
42	Am I The Boss I Wish I Had?
49	Do I Spend As Much Time Praising As I Do Correcting?
57	Is It More Important To Be Right Or Do Right?
66	Why Do You Think You'd Be A Good Fit For Our Company?
80	As A Manager, Why Should Leadership Training Be Important To Me?
90	Is The Customer Always Right?
96	I'm Just As Good, Why Didn't I Get That Job?
103	Why Am I Up To My Neck In Alligators, When I Came To Drain The Swamp?
112	What Can I Do To Increase The Level Of Customer Service We're Providing?
121	What Else Can I Do?
130	As A Retailer, What's Our Purpose? What's Our Job?

1

NOW I'M A MANAGER, WHAT THINGS SHOULD I DO DIFFERENTLY?

PUNCH-IN IDEAS: My problem was I never asked myself this question. When I reported to work on my very first day as a part-timer, my manager told me, "Work hard, keep busy and you'll do fine." And this 'work hard' philosophy was ingrained in me from that moment on. How quick could I get the delivery unloaded? How much work could I do in a shift? Since I wanted to be successful, all I had to do was work harder and faster than other people. So that's what I did. I was young, I was naive, and I could get a lot done in a short amount of time. I was good ... really good! Then I got promoted!

As a newly promoted department manager, one of the biggest mistakes I made was misunderstanding how to "lead by example." Now don't get me wrong, I still believe in "leading by example," in fact, I regard it as one of the most important leadership qualities to embrace ... I just took it a little too far.

You see, as a regular employee I often felt my managers didn't do their share of the normal every-day work. They took longer breaks then normal, they would sit around talking about things instead of working, etc. Now maybe all employees feel that way, I don't know, but when I got promoted, I didn't want my employees to think of me like that. That's why I decided I was going to work harder than any employee AND I wouldn't ask anyone to do something I wasn't willing to do myself.

Sound good? I thought so. I believed once my employees saw how hard I worked, they would join in and follow my example. I assumed this was the way to be a successful manager. Well, it took me a while to learn my lesson, as things didn't work out quite the way I expected.

Oh, yes, my employees saw how hard I worked and how quickly I moved to make sure things got done. But what did they do? Well, since all of the work was getting done, they just continued at their same pace and let me keep working as fast as I could go. In fact, although I never was able to prove it, I think a few of them actually slowed down some just to see how much harder and faster I could go. And of course, since I wanted to prove I, the new manager, could handle the situation, I kept going as hard and as fast as I could.

I understand now, this situation isn't uncommon among retailers, ... a hard, fast-working employee is promoted to manager, because ... well, he was hard-working and able to get so much accomplished. One day he's a regular employee, doing his own thing, then "POOF," the next he's the manager. So what does he do? Well, he got promoted because he was a hard working employee who could get a lot of work done, so now he becomes an even harder working manager trying to do even more.

But this just causes future problems ... because although this new manager may be able to keep going at this hectic pace for a while, rarely does it last for very long. In fact, one of two things usually happens. (1) Sooner or later that fast hard-working manager gets frustrated, worn down or completely burned out. Or (2), he's in a small enough volume store or department where he can get most of the work done by himself or with just a few people. Then, a year or so down the line he gets promoted to a bigger volume store, and WHAM, he fails miserably because there's no way he can do all of the required work at this bigger location.

So what's the solution? Well, the first and most important point a new manager must understand is ...

> **"... employees are judged by what they can personally accomplish, while managers are judged by what they can accomplish through others."**

Now it's important to stop and think about this for a minute ... as an employee we're judged by how well we personally do a job ... how well we unload a delivery, work a grill or take care of a counter. But the minute we become a manager, we're no longer judged by what we can personally do, instead, we're judged by what our employees, collectively, do ... how clean and sanitary they keep the department ... how quickly they get the cars through the drive-thru or how well-merchandised they keep the displays.

> **Once we become managers, our success stops being about what WE do ... and becomes more about what our EMPLOYEES do.**

Now this can be a scary reckoning, because it means our success or failure, as managers, depends completely on how well our people perform. Now that's quite a change from being an employee where we have direct control over our own fate ... now it depends on how well others do. It also means if we want to be successful managers, we should be looking for ways to help our employees do their jobs as well as possible.

No, I didn't say "do their jobs for them," I said, "help them do their jobs." And there's a big difference between the two. The truth is, we can't do it for them ... we have to do it through them. That's what being a manager, and more importantly, what being a leader, is all about. This was a difficult lesson for me to learn.

Like many other managers, I kept seeing these as two separate issues. I used to think of it as ...

... "I'm doing a great job as a manager, but these people are sure doing a poor job as employees."
or
"If I just had better employees, I know I could be a better manager."

Have you ever felt this way? Well, those were the kinds of things I felt. The point I had to learn was this, ... there is no separation ... there is no "I'm good and they are bad" scenario. The truth is ...

> **If my employees are under-performing, then I'm not doing the job I was promoted to do.**
> **It's my RESPONSIBILITY.**
> **It's just that simple.**

Now again, I know you may not want to hear this, I know I didn't. I also realize it may be difficult to accept because it goes against our own internal self-management philosophy as well as what we're told as employees, but that old THE HARDER YOU WORK, THE MORE SUCCESSFUL YOU'LL BE philosophy doesn't work, when talking about a manager. The reality is, once you're a manager ...

Your Success or Failure Depends Much More On What Your People Do, Than On What You Do!

As a manager, it's not about YOU anymore, it's about YOUR PEOPLE. This is one of the basic truths I learned later in my career which I wish I understood when I was a store-level manager.

And as a basic truth, it leads us directly to an important question ... a question we should be asking ourselves over and over ...

"What things can we do to help our employees WANT to do a better job and THEN be more successful when they try?"

Well first, very few of us are natural-born leaders. So if you're like most people, myself included, it takes time to learn how to effectively lead, mobilize, and inspire people ... and that's okay. But it's important to, at least, ask the question and think about what we can do to answer it.

So, to help get you started, here are five basic things you can start doing right now that will set the foundation for you to become a better, smarter, more effective leader. You may already be doing a couple of these, and that's good ... but take the time to think about how you can maximize these areas.

First — Be Trustworthy, Honest & Open

I know this may sound like a simple thing, but it continually amazes me how many of today's managers are not. Maybe you've had one or two of them. Instead, make it a point to show people, through your daily behaviors, what it means to have integrity, a strong work ethic, and an unyielding commitment to your organization's mission and values. Now that's the kind of person employees will believe in, that's the kind of person they will follow.

- **Walk Your Talk**, don't say one thing and then act another
- **Be Ethical**, no one likes a corrupt boss ...
- **Don't Blame Others** for your mistakes ...
- **Keep People Informed** about what's going on, have meetings, talk to your people, don't hide things

Second — Learn How to Influence, Not Dictate

Forcing employees to do things, causes bitterness and resentment. Learn to influence employees by having open and honest conversations about 'why' certain things should be done certain ways. I once heard it said, *"Employee retention is not about keeping bodies, it's about keeping their minds and hearts."*

Third — Become a Better Listener

Focus on understanding the messages your employees send to you. People can tell when someone isn't listening, and it's insulting. Demonstrate that you care what others think, feel, and have to say by how you listen and react to their comments.

Fourth — Provide Encouragement

It's been proven time and time again, <u>positive encouragement</u> gets better results than <u>constructive criticism</u>. But that's a message we're rarely taught at the retail level. So look for opportunities to celebrate your employees' achievements.

Fifth — Focus More on Your Employees than Yourself

Treat employees with dignity, respect and courtesy. Respect their time and work to get them what they need to be successful at their job. When appropriate, get them involved by delegating responsibilities and the necessary authority to accomplish certain tasks. Learn to take more of the criticism, and less of the credit.

Those are five basic ways to start your transformation from being a manager to becoming a leader. And remember ...

'You can be APPOINTED a manager, but you have to EARN the name, leader.'

And this name comes with a numerous responsibilities, one of which is for you to continue growing and improving. So as you begin this process, don't be too hard when you make a mistake or two. It's going to happen. Just learn from them and move on!

— Chapter 1 Notes —

PUNCH-OUT THOUGHTS:

- *When was the last time you actually explained to your employees about what's going on in the company or brought them up-to-date on the department sales, profits and goals? When is the best time to do this?*

- *Do you think your employees view you as an honest and fair person who 'walks his talk?' How could you find out?*

- *Do your employees know you care about them as people, and not just as workers? Are you sure? What have you done to make sure they know?*

- *In your operation, do you spend more time looking for things that need to be corrected or things that should be praised? Is this the way you want to be regarded?*

11
WHAT CAN I DO TO HELP ME LEARN, ADVANCE AND GROW?

PUNCH-IN IDEAS: I was always curious ... I wanted to know more ... I wanted to be better ... I wanted to see if there was a better way to do something. I still remember this day just like it was yesterday. I was really upset at the time, but as I look back, I see where it helped motivate me to get out of that store and move up.

As we discussed in the last chapter, it's not so uncommon for a person to be a hard-working employee one day, then "POOF," the next he's the manager. And, generally speaking, the new manager has received little to no leadership or managerial training. But, from management's perspective this does not relieve the new manager from delivering the expected results. So what does he do?

He was a hard working employee who could get a lot of work done, so now he becomes a even harder working manager trying to do more. Instead of working to get the job done through his people, he works even harder to get the job done himself. This is a common mistake ... and it's very natural.

That's where personal leadership and managerial education comes into play. Today there are plenty of general programs out there which can be used to help us through this process. **In fact, investing in yourself can be one of the best investments you will ever make.**

I remember starting one of these programs while I was that young department manager at a major supermarket company in Chicago. The lesson I was studying explained that if I wanted to 'think' clearer and more creatively, I had to train my mind to do so. The rationale behind this concept was that singers have to train their voices in order to sing ... athletes have to train their muscles in order to be able to compete at a high level ... and if we want to think clearer and more creatively, then naturally, we have to train our minds to do so.

Now in order to accomplish this, the program suggested I begin a simple daily fifteen minute exercise. I was to find a quiet place to sit down and relax ... close my eyes, pick one subject, and try to remove everything else (sounds, ideas, images, etc.) from my mind. The basic premise was learning to focus on one subject for 15 minutes.

Now, I remember being on break one afternoon, sitting on some cases piled up in my supermarket's backroom. I had my eyes closed and was diligently trying to go through this thought-process when my store manager walked by and asked what I was doing. Embarrassed, I quickly explained about this training exercise and the concept of learning to think at a higher degree. He stopped me short and responded,

> **"Buck, you obviously don't understand, you're not paid to think, you're paid to do what you're told."**

Now, I don't know whether or not he was having a bad day and I don't know if he really felt this way but, I do know I never forgot that moment. In fact, his remark helped change me in two ways ... first, it helped motivate me to keep learning and growing because I didn't like the idea of getting paid just, "to do what I was told," ... especially since I knew he would be one of those doing the telling. And second, if he and other store managers truly felt this way, then I couldn't just take what they said and believe it, ... I was going to have to be better than that and that meant I had to learn to think for myself.

I viewed 'learning, growing and thinking' as providing me a path to move forward, to get better, to advance up through the ranks. As a result, I continued the process even as a top executive and later with my own company. Of course, once I reached that level I no longer had to sit on cases in the backroom of a supermarket in order to practice 'thinking.'

So what's my answer to "What things can I do to help me advance and grow?" Without a doubt, and with no hesitation my immediate response would be ... to THINK and to CREATE.

I always laugh when people tell me, "I'm not creative," or "I'm not the intellectual type" somehow believing that people are born creative or that intellectual types are more able to think or somehow consider other alternatives. That's ridiculous.

I have yet to meet a non-creative person or someone that can't consider other alternatives. The truth is, most people don't think they have the ability because they just don't try. Or, they try once and things don't quite work out the way they thought, so they never try again.

So how did I learn to think and create? Well, I'm going back to one of the first things mentioned at the beginning of this book, ask questions ... or better yet, ask the right questions! If you're a store or department manager here are examples of some questions you should ask.

- What new thing can I do this week to attract more customers into my department or store?

- What can I do to get more people to buy this particular item/product?
- What can we do to make it more enjoyable for our customers to shop this department/store?
- How can I build a display that will get more customers to stop, look and buy off it?

Here's what you do ... find someplace where you can have a little peace and quiet ... clear your mind of other interruptions ... then ask yourself one of these questions. Then, start thinking of ways you could answer the question ... things you could do, things you could try. Write down your ideas ... and don't worry if you think a few might sound a little crazy right now. Just write them down.

Now, after you write down as many ideas as you can think of, select two or three of the best ones and write next to them, what you would need, how it would work, who else could help with it, what kind of time frame would be involved, etc. Just take a few minutes to write these few particulars down.

Okay, now comes the two most important parts of this whole process ... first, you must select the one idea you think will work the best. No, you can't select two, only one. Make a choice. You can do that. And second, after you've made your choice, take the first couple of steps to make it happen. No, don't wait until tomorrow, do it now, start the process. It doesn't have to be a lot. Maybe you just call the person who you want to help you and let them know what the two or you will be doing. Maybe it's just ordering some material. Maybe it's just cleaning up the area where that new display will go. It may be different in each circumstance, but you must at least start the process right now. Do something, make progress, get it started, take the first step NOW!

Don't worry about it not working, or that the idea may not be good enough. You're going to make a mistake every now and then ... we all do. I had a great idea one St. Pats Day to put green food coloring into our ham salad. I thought it would be a great way to add some color into our deli counter. Hmmm ... what I found out was green Ham Salad doesn't look too appetizing. In fact, almost any meat item that's green doesn't look too good. Anyway, we ended up throwing away over 50 pounds of green Ham Salad that holiday. Oh well, I never tried that one again.

So be willing to investment in yourself, continue to try, continue to learn and grow. That investment may require money for specific leadership and management CD programs, books and DVD's and it may require time in order to complete these programs, read new material, etc. Do whatever it takes, but it's important that you continue to fill your mind with new ideas, different thoughts and controversial opinions. That's what I mean by 'thinking.' You have to make a conscience effort and be willing to consider other ideas, other options, other ways of doing something.

As a manager and leader, never resign yourself to just "doing what you're told." Your ability to THINK ... to QUESTION ... and to CREATE is what makes you unique ... it's what makes you SPECIAL. Plus, it's these same characteristics that make each of our employees SPECIAL, too. Therefore, we should strive to build an environment where our people can prosper and grow, not be stifled.

And again, ... don't be afraid to invest in YOUR development, in YOUR growth, in YOU. Remember ...

> **... if you aren't willing to invest in yourself, how can you expect anyone else to?**

— Chapter 2 Notes —

PUNCH-OUT THOUGHTS:

- *What programs do you have in effect right now to help you improve in some way? What are you waiting for? How can you be better next month or next year, if you don't start right now?*

> There's a big difference between ten years of experience and one year of experience repeated ten times.

- *For us in retail, it's so easy to get caught in the trap of just repeating things from one year to the next. You know what I mean ... each year we repeat the same things as we go through the cycle for Independence Day, Back-To-School, Labor Day, Halloween, Thanksgiving, Christmas, New Years, Super Bowl, Valentine's Day, Easter, Memorial Day, Independence Day, Back-To-School, Labor Day and on and on, over and over again.*

    It's so easy to get caught in the 'holiday cycle' and keep doing the same things over and over. But don't let that happen. Make yourself look for ways to get better, to improve. Don't just take that 'one year of experience' and keep repeating it. Learn to create, work to get better.

- *In this chapter we provide examples of a few 'right questions' you could ask yourself as a way to begin to learn and create. What other questions could you ask?*

You could also ask these questions of your employees as a way to bring them into the creation process. This helps build your work forces' ownership and engagement as well as expand the number of answers you have to solve the problem. Think about this, it's a win-win for everyone but how could you do it?

AM I PAYING YOU RIGHT NOW?

PUNCH-IN IDEAS: As a manager, most of us have had to deal with an employee or two who seem to waste an inappropriate amount of time. A few years ago a friend of mine mentioned her solution to me and I thought it was a great approach to an age old problem. I just wish I had known about it back when I was in the stores.

We've all found ourselves in this situation at one time or another ... an employee shows up a few minutes late, punches in, puts on a uniform or apron, takes a bathroom break, talks to friend or two, and then 15 to 20 minutes after their start time, they actually start working. Or better yet, how about the employee who always seems to be talking on their cell phone or texting during the work day?

Based on the people and companies I work with, this particular problem seems to be happening more and more as social media becomes a bigger and more prominent part of our everyday life. Of course, as we all know, this really isn't a social media problem, it's a management problem, one that's actually existed from the beginning of time.

In fact, I have it on good authority that researchers digging in the caves of Borneo have found documented evidence that the first such case occurred around 2000 BC. It seems a caveman, Ugg, hired another cavemen to help him manufacture clubs for the caveman tribe. No, Ugg didn't have to worry about his employee talking on a cell phone, but, whenever Ugg wasn't watching, this guy liked to draw images on the cave walls. Obviously, based on what we see today, Ugg wasn't paying too close attention to what was actually going on.

So what do we do when we see this happen? What's the best way to handle a situation like this? Maybe the question is, 'What would Ugg have done?'

Well, there are many ways to address this issue, some good and some not so good, but the first point to understand is this ... the issue MUST be addressed, and it needs to be addressed IMMEDIATELY. Like most people, it took Ugg a good amount of time to learn this ... and while he waited, his club manufacturing business really suffered. But eventually he realized he couldn't ignore the issue, it wouldn't go away ... and as a manager, even a lowly manager like Ugg, he had to address it. Period!

So what's the big deal about addressing this issue right away? Couldn't you just bide your time, see how things progress and if things don't improve then address it?

Well first, if it isn't addressed right away, the issue will only get bigger. Oh, it may not happen immediately, but over time it will grow. Today it may be one person losing 5 or 10 minutes, but two or three months from now it could easily be three or four people losing 15 to 20 minutes. The problem with letting things go is that employees begin to feel it's an acceptable practice ... it's the standard that's been set ... and once that happens, it becomes even more difficult to stop.

Second, employees need to be made aware and occasionally reminded that within the work environment there's an exchange of value constantly taking place. Management has agreed to pay a certain amount of money (measured in dollars, benefits, holiday pay, etc.) for a certain amount of work effort (measured in hours, results, etc.) from the employee. Both parties have agreed to this exchange of value, and it's the responsibility of each to maintain and uphold it.

So okay, what do we do? How do we handle a situation when we feel an employee isn't holding up their share of the value exchange?

A few years ago I was having a similar discussion with a business friend of mine (no, it wasn't Ugg), and she admitted this was a problem that plagued her for a good part of her retail management career. In fact, it wasn't until her fifth or sixth year in management that she discovered an effective way to address the issue. Here's what worked for her.

Any time she found an employee who was 'on the clock,' so to speak, and who was not doing a work task ... in other words, an employee who was supposed to be working but was involved in some other non-working personal activity, she would immediately ask one simple, straightforward question, ...

"Am I Paying You Right Now?"

She never yelled it or made a scene with it, she just asked the question in a simple and direct manner. She told me she did it this way because she wanted her employees to know she wasn't joking around.

She said once she asked the question, people would immediately stop what they were doing, pause a second or two, answer a quiet, "Yes, You Are!" and then sheepishly start back doing a work task. Eventually, she added, whenever employees saw her approaching they'd make comments like, "Yes, you're paying me right now, and I'm working!"

Now, would I use this concept the first time I found someone doing personal work while on my time? Probably not, but I really don't know. I guess it depends on a lot of things like the circumstances, the particulars and the specific person. With my management style, I'd first probably try to explain, why they shouldn't be doing personal work and how important it is for them to keep working. But, if I found I was having even the smallest problem with employees doing personal work on the clock, I'd come out firing with this question.

I love this approach and feel it's a great way to focus attention on the basic premise — when employees are on the clock, they're getting paid, and that means they should be working. This is a message our employees need to understand and we should be telling them this every day. This simple question actually addresses many employer-employee dynamics. Let me show you what I mean!

IT'S A QUESTION!

First of all, we're not making a statement, we're not demanding anything, we're just asking a simple question. And because it's a question, that puts us in control, it puts us in charge of the conversation. Plus, there's strong social pressure for the other person to answer it. That reinforces our position of power and control while putting pressure on the employee.

Now of course, there's only one answer to this question, and we all know what that is ... 'yes.' So when they agree that "yes, you are paying me right now," they're admitting they're getting paid for whatever they happen to be doing at that exact moment. And truthfully, they know, and everyone else knows if they should be getting paid to do that or not. The whole thing is simple, straight-forward and self-explanatory.

IT ADDRESSES THE PROBLEM HEAD ON!

Second, these six powerful words, "Am I Paying You Right Now?" hit straight at the issue. There's no confusion as to what the issue may or may not be ... there's no doubt if it should be an issue or not ... and there's no misunderstanding about how important it is. There are no grey areas, it's strictly black and white ... and most of the time it's only black. There's no dodging that reality, there's no side-tracking the message ... it's straight forward and right to the point ... "Am I Paying You Right Now?"

One other point here, as I said above, "most of the time it's only black," ... but it is possible for the situation to be white. For example, what if the employee answers back, "Yes, you're paying me but I'm on break right now." Now, all of a sudden, everything's changed. A proper response to that may be something like, "I'm really glad to hear that because I was having trouble believing you would be this way when you're supposed to be working. That's just not you."

MANAGER vs EMPLOYEE DIFFERENCE

Third, by asking this question I'm also re-establishing my authority as the manager. And as such, I not only have the right to ask you this, ... but also the right to hold you accountable for this. That's my job as the manager. This kind of question sets those guidelines and reaffirms our individual responsibilities. It says I have the right to make sure you're holding up your end of the bargain, just as you do to make sure I'm correctly reimbursing you. These go hand-in-hand, that's part of the employee/employer relationship. As such, since I'm paying you right now, I have a right to know what I am getting in return.

RIGHT NOW! PINPOINTS THIS EXACT MOMENT

Fourth, by asking the question in this manner, we're focussing on this exact moment, this exact point in time. You see, it doesn't make any difference if you worked hard yesterday, this morning or an hour ago ... the question is, "Am I paying you RIGHT NOW?" If I am, then "What am I getting RIGHT NOW from your effort?" Because, if I'm paying you RIGHT NOW, but I'm not getting anything RIGHT NOW in return, then we have a problem.

That's why the "Right Now" ending is so important to this question. It eliminates all other times, and focusses our attention to this specific moment.

EXCHANGE OF MONEY FOR EFFORT

Fifth, by asking, "Am I paying you right now," there's another message, a more subliminal one that surfaces ... both of us have agreed to a fair exchange of money for effort/work put for. Consequently, if either of us are not holding up our side of the deal, then we're at fault, we're guilty, we're falling short of our commitment. No one likes to be made aware they're not following through the way they have agreed to do. That's embarrassing.

IT ESTABLISHES THE COUNTERPOINT

Sixth, and this may be the most important point. By asking "Am I paying you right now?" we're also implying that "Maybe I shouldn't be paying you right now!" and "Maybe I shouldn't be paying you for what you're doing at this specific moment?" It makes this a possibility ... it opens up the idea that there could be a repercussion based on what you are NOT doing right now.

Am I Paying You Right Now?

It's the right question ... asked the right way! I just wish I had started using it years ago ... it would have made my life so much easier. Try it the next time this kind of situation happens to you and see how well it works.

PUNCH-OUT THOUGHTS: Some people believe, we should never ask a question that can be answered with a yes or no. Instead, we should only ask 'open-ended' questions ... questions that require a more in-depth answer. I don't necessarily agree with that notion. I have found there are times when either style can be quite effective, it depends more on the circumstances than anything else. For example, here are two ways the question in our scenario could be asked:

Am I paying you right now?
or
Why am I paying you right now?

The first question, "Am I paying you right now?" can be answered with a yes or no response but it still insinuates that I probably shouldn't be paying you. It makes this basic point with the person who is asked while letting them know, "I'm paying attention. I have an expectation."

The second question, "Why am I paying you right now?" requires more of a response than just a yes or no. In addition, this is a much more direct, tougher and in-your-face question. Some people may take offense or feel threatened by it and that can be good or bad depending on your intentions.

As I mentioned though, the question you choose will depend on the circumstances, the person, the place, etc., but for me, initially I would be asking the first one ("Am I paying you right now?). This brings the situation to the forefront, lets the employee know there's a problem, and they need to fix it. But, I also know, if I found this situation was not improving, and I had multiple occurrences, I would start asking the second question which takes this situation to a more serious level.

— Chapter 3 Notes —

- *Do you have employees who seem to waste a lot of time while on the job? Are these reoccurring problems that don't seem to be getting any better? Explain.*

- *What other ways have you tried to address this situation?*

- *How do you think your other employees feel watching a peer waste time?*

- *What things can you do to make an impression concerning the importance of not wasting time?*

IV

WHAT IS YOUR MAIN JOB TONIGHT?

PUNCH-IN IDEAS: As retailers, we're all taught to leave assignment lists for the next crew to handle. In my case, this was especially true for the night crew. As the day manager left, he would usually leave a list of tasks that needed to be completed during the evening hours so the shop looked its best at the start of the new day. One of the first lessons I learned as a part-time retail clerk was ... the items on the list MUST be completed before I left, but there would be NO over-time AND I had to be out the door at the appointed time.

As a manager, when you exit your store at the end of the day, do you leave a list of things you want completed before some of the others can leave?

As a part-timer, I remember getting that type of list every night from my manager as he walked out the door. Of course, since overtime was a definite "no no," we had to make sure everything was completed and wrapped up by closing time. Some nights the list would be long, other nights there would only be a few things on it ... but no matter what, we had to finish the tasks on the list. Plus, and it went without saying, we also had to take care of any
customers that came to the counter wanting to be served.

Now, this doesn't sound too complicated, but here's what would inevitably happen. We'd get started doing the tasks on the list, and then a customer would come up and we'd have to stop and take care of them. Then we'd go back to our items list, another customer would arrive, and we'd have to stop again. Obviously, this didn't have to happen many times before our attitude became ...

> **"I wish these customers would leave me alone so I could get my work done."**

In other words, our job became the list of "tasks" we had to complete ... and "customers" became an interruption that made it harder for us to complete our job.

Does this sound familiar? Have you ever been in this situation? Have you ever left your people in situations like this? Do you think if employees had this type of attitude, a customer might even be able to sense their frustration and impatience?

Plus, it didn't stop there because what do you think the manager did as soon as he arrived in the store the next morning? Yep, he'd grab the list and start checking to make sure each item had been finished. He would then compliment or complain to the crew based on how well the items on the list had been accomplished. And, by the way, I don't ever remember him asking, "how well did you take care of last night's customers?" or "Did you have a lot of customers?" As a part-timer I remember thinking, *to him, the customers are just an after-thought and the tasks are really what's important.*

Now I understand the need to leave lists. As a manager and supervisor, I left a lot of them myself. Plus, I understand the importance of making sure the department is set the way it needs to be for the next day's crew or opening. But I also know it's possible to be so focussed on completing a list of tasks, that we forget our job is really satisfying the customer. And I definitely know that's not the message we want to send to our employees.

So what do we do? How do we solve this? How do we help our employees understand the importance of all of these areas? Here are three points to consider.

First, there must be an overall understanding by everyone in the department that our first and foremost responsibility is taking care of our customers. There can be NO exceptions, NO other considerations ... the customer is first and foremost. ALL The Time! Every time! PERIOD!

And employees need to understand that putting customers first requires more than just saying it - which leads us to the second point.

> **There are certain 'tasks' that must be completed because by completing them, it makes taking care of the customer easier to do.**

Now, have I really confused you with that one? Let me explaining. How can we effectively demonstrate to our customers that we really want to take care of them if we have a dirty display case, ... if the equipment isn't cleaned, ... if the floors aren't swept and mopped regularly, ... if our products aren't fresh, and so on? Think about how you would feel going into a retail shop and finding those kinds of things and then some clerk tries to tell you that they really care about you ... that "you're number one" ... and that they want to make sure you are satisfied? Would you believe them? Would you let them take care of you?

You see, what's important here is for our employees to understand that by completing these tasks, we are actually demonstrating to our customers that we care about them and want to serve them better.

Now this may seem a small point, but it's a tremendously important one because it explains the 'why' ... why we do these tasks. And that's the key. We're not doing these tasks because that's our job ... we're doing these tasks because completing them helps us do our job of servicing customers better ... and that's the distinction.

We stock cases, mop floors, straighten counters, sanitize equipment, clean shelves and all the other tasks because it helps us serve our greater purpose of taking better care of the customer.

And of course, the third point is, as a manager, we must show a level of acceptance if the shop is left less than perfect whenever the shift has an over abundance of customers. This is also very important because it demonstrates to our employees that we, as managers, really do place customer service at the top of the list ... we really do walk-our-talk. And believe me, employees watch very closely to see how this type of situation is handled.

One of the first rules of management is ...

... we get what we reward
or
we get what we pay attention to ...

... and this is so true. So if we only pay attention to or reward (through compliments, praise, etc.) the fact the tasks on the list are completed, then that's what we will get ... completed check lists. But, on the other hand, if we pay attention to and check to make sure our customers are being well taken care of, even at times at the expense of completed check lists, our employees will give better and better customer service.

So let's review our overall message here ... "yes, the tasks we do are important ... but they are important because by completing them we are providing a better environment in which to accomplish our primary responsibility ... the responsibility of taking care of our customers' problems."

— Chapter 4 Notes —

PUNCH-OUT THOUGHTS:
- *What kind of lists do you leave for your employees?*

- *When you report back to work the next day, do you pay more attention to the completion of tasks on your list or the customers served? Are you sure? Do your employees see it that way?*

- *What can you do to impress upon your employees the importance of servicing customers even when you're not there?*

- *What things can you put in place to track the number of customers your employees serve when you're not there?*

- *Is there another way to track and monitor your customer transactions?*

V
DO YOU UNDERSTAND WHY ?

PUNCH-IN IDEAS: As I grew up, authority figures didn't tell you WHY, they just told you WHAT to do and HOW quickly it needed to be done. I can just imagine asking my old high school football coach, "Excuse me, Mr. Scott, would you explain why you want us to run toboggan hill before we start the dreaded "pig in the middle" drill? Oh yes, that would have gone over real well. Hmmm ... I guess things have changed a lot since then.

Recently, I read a research report which stated, *"Companies that manage people right will outperform companies that don't by 30% to 40%."*
Well, that doesn't seem too surprising. We all would agree that it's easier to work for a good manager than a poor one. But, what does 'managing people right' mean and who gets to make that determination ... the manager or the employee?

Well first, as far as who makes the determination, the answer is neither and both. In fact, that determination is going to be made by numerous people including the manager's boss, the manager himself, and, of course, the employees. Each of these will have different criteria for determining whether or not 'people are being managed right,' but all three viewpoints have to come together to form the overall evaluation.

Now, as to what does 'managing people right' mean, many elements come into play and have to be considered here. As an example, 'managing people right' would have to include personal traits such as the manager being truthful, respectful and fair with the employees. In addition we also have to consider managerial elements such as providing recognition, motivation and leadership qualities. And, of course, we'd also like managers to help employees grow and advance within the company structure.

Another element that has become extremely important with employees, and as such, constitutes a direct link to higher employee performance is the ability and willingness of managers to explain, "WHY."

> **Years ago we thought it was enough to just tell our employees 'what" to do and 'how' to do it.**

We have since discovered that employee performance improves dramatically (which improves sales and profits) when they 'buy in' to the directive ... in other words, when they understand 'why' this particular course of action is needed and what is hoped to be accomplished by it.

This was again reinforced to me recently when my oldest son, a football coach at a local Dallas area high school, commented how the players execute much better when the coaches take the time, to explain up-front, **WHY** they want them to do something or **WHY** they want it done a certain way.

When I asked him about it he responded, "we've found when we take the time to explain to the players *why* we're running this particular defense, or *why* we're putting in this new play, or *why* we believe this blocking scheme will work ... the players execute at a much higher level than when we just say, "here's what we want you to do."

He added, "today's players want to believe what we're telling them will work. So, as coaches, we have to "sell" them on that fact. The important part of this whole point is once they believe in what we're telling them, they focus better on exactly what they need to do. And as a result we can actually document, on video, how the execution level shows dramatic improvement. So, explaining WHY has become important to all of our coaches."

Now, the minute he started talking, I found myself laughing on the inside because for years I had experienced the same results in the retail sector, and yet, here was my son lecturing me on what he had recently 'discovered' in sports. Of course, I also had an immediate flash back to my old high school football coach.

First, I can honestly say without any reservation, "I don't remember anyone ever having the guts to ask my old football coach "why" about anything he told us to do." We all knew that would have been suicide. Second, I went on and played Division I college basketball for some very well known coaches, and no one ever asked them "why" either. Again, that would have been unthinkable.

So, I guess times have really changed ... yet, I'm not always so sure. I wonder if it's that the "times" have changed as much, or is it that we understand so much more about behavior that we're changing our approach so we get better results? And I'm not too sure we aren't the same way ourselves.

Answer this ... Would you work harder on a project where you were told ...

... just what to do?

or a project where you were told ...

... what to do, why the project and your particular job were important, how you fit and what you had to do to make the project successful?

Could it be possible that our employees want us to tell them why, too? Is it possible we'd get better execution if we took time each week to exactly explain to them why we're building the type of displays, or why these items are priced the way they are, or why a particular sales or gross profit level is so important?

By explaining **WHY,** we're helping them become part of the program and its execution. Through this understanding comes an increased willingness to act as well as an increased accountability. And isn't this what we want from our employees?

So as a combined lesson from Human Nature 101 and Common Sense 101, there's a much better chance people will be motivated and give their enthusiastic support if they understand the reason behind a goal, assignment, or decision instead of just the goal itself.

Make it a point to start explaining 'why' and see if it doesn't work for you, too.

— Chapter 5 Notes —

PUNCH-OUT THOUGHTS:
- *When was the last time you actually explained any 'whys' of your operation to your employees? If you did, what kind of questions and results did you get? If not, why not?*

- *What's one important 'why' you'd like your employees to understand right now? Period Sales? Margins? Quotas? Deliveries?*

- *If explaining why seems to be too much trouble, think about how you'd like to know 'why' on directives from your boss. Just because he may not be explaining them to you, doesn't mean you shouldn't tell you people why.*

VI

AM I THE BOSS I WISH I HAD?

PUNCH-IN IDEAS: In my career I've had good bosses, I've had some not-so-good ones. I've had bosses I respected and believed in and I've had bosses I wouldn't trust as far as I could throw them. And one of the most important points I've learned is, if you work for a boss you like, trust and respect ... learn from that relationship and value it highly.

In my retail career, I worked for four different companies and had numerous bosses: some good, some bad ... two of them I would call great; they served as mentors and role models. ONE though, was an absolute terror. Let me tell you a story.

As V.P. of our Service Departments, I was preparing for the yearly meeting with the V.P.'s of our four divisions and their executive staffs. We were implementing a new reporting system and wanted the Divisional V.P.'s to see how it worked. My boss and I had been going over this system for the last week or so, but had major disagreements on how the information should be gathered. I felt there were major flaws in his interpretation but I wasn't able to convince him to let me make the adjustments. Finally, he just told me, "this is the way the system is going to work, so get over it."

As it turned out, I didn't get five minutes into the next day's presentation, before the Divisional V.P.'s started interrupting me to point out why they didn't think the system would work. As proof, they began to give me the exact reasons I had been giving my boss the whole previous week. And although I didn't agree with it or feel comfortable with it, I continued to support my boss' position, even though it was obvious the V.P.'s weren't happy.

After about 15 minutes of this back and forth discussion, my boss finally stood up at the side of the room and said, *"Buck, it's obvious the system you're proposing isn't going to work. And frankly, I'm a little disappointed you couldn't see this beforehand."* Then he turned to the divisional people and continued, *"But don't worry, I'll get with him later today, make the necessary changes and we'll have everything ready to go within 24 hours."*

I remember standing at the front of the room thinking, *"okay, what just happened? ... not only had my boss thrown me under the bus in front of the Operations V.P.'s, but he had actually driven it back and forth over me four or five times before driving away."* I was furious, and was trying to determine if I should say something right there or wait until later. But I held my temper, sat back down and we finished the meeting.

Later that day, when my boss and I met, I let him know how I felt about that morning's discussion. I thought he might make some type of apology to try and smooth things out but instead, his only response was something like, *"it really doesn't make any difference now who wanted to do what or who liked which system, ... the key is just to fix the problem and get the correct system in place."* I remember thinking, *"Yeah, maybe it doesn't make any difference to you, but it sure makes a difference to me!"*

This is just one of many examples of how this person operated. I never felt I could trust him, depend on him or rely on anything he said. It was a nightmare for me.

So from a leadership perspective, I had some good role models and some poor ones. But I quickly learned one main point, 'having a title or a leadership position, and 'actually being a leader' are two completely different things.'

Here's the way I look at it. The position you hold today is something you were appointed to ... something you became eligible for by being a good performer in the past. What you did "yesterday," as an employee, helped you get the title or classification you hold today. And that's exactly what your position is, a title ... a classification.

But, being a true leader is much different. "Leader" is a descriptor – a label that is EARNED through specific behaviors. It's based on what you do today, and what you will do tomorrow – not what's printed on your name tag.

So, how do you become a good leader? Although there are hundreds of books written on the 'do's' and 'don'ts' of leadership, when I looked back and reviewed the bosses I had, I realized there were five traits consistent among the ones I considered good leaders. I also realized not only were these same traits missing from the boss I considered poor, but in many cases, he did the exact opposite.

Now, you may have different criteria that are important to you, but here are the five things these managers did that made me feel they were good and great leaders. See if these areas are as important to you as they are to me.

ONE: They Walked Their Talk

... they did what they said they would do. I felt I could trust them because they practiced what they preached ... they had integrity. No, we didn't always agree, and they didn't let me do everything I wanted, but I knew once we walked out of that room, they would do what we agreed to do ... and I made sure I did the same. There were no surprises.

TWO: They Wanted Their People To Succeed

... they helped promote the accomplishments of their people up and down the company chain. If they made a mistake, which did happen every now and then, they would own up to it, they didn't blame someone else. In fact, at times it actually seemed they took more responsibility when things went wrong and less of the credit when things went right.

THREE: They Made Me Feel Important

... they kept me informed about what was going on in the company. They didn't hide facts ... they made me feel I was contributing to the organization's success, and that made me feel important to the company. And, another one of the biggest things, they gave me their time ... I was able to get to them when I needed them.

FOUR: They Cared About People As Individuals

... they built a team atmosphere. They didn't pit one person against another. They seemed to care about me, as an individual, not just as an employee. They made it a point to ask about my family and took the time to speak and get to know them when the opportunities arose.

FIVE: They Gave Me the Opportunity To Succeed

... they worked to get me the things I needed (tools, training, support, room, etc.) to do the best I could. If I asked, they tried to get me those things ... no, they weren't always able to make it happen ... but they tried. And that was very important to me. One other area that impressed me was they didn't hold me back or tell me why things wouldn't work. Yes, they had hurdles I had to get over, and objectives I had to meet, but they encouraged me to keep going and to try. I always felt they had my back ... I wasn't alone.

Now, you can go on-line and find any number of quotes about Leadership. One of my favorites is **"Giving orders is not leadership, giving hope is."** I love this quote because people want to believe they can succeed ... they want to believe they will be successful. And as a leader we can give them that hope, and then help them make it come true. That's what my good bosses did for me, and what I tried to do for my employees. And isn't that what we should be doing for our employees today?

One other thought about this ... most of the time when we talk about what leaders should or shouldn't do, we like to compare the answers to our own bosses' performance ... you know, to see if our bosses are measuring up to how 'good' we feel bosses should act.

This time though, why not take those five points and compare them to your own management style. Are you doing these things? Are you thinking and acting in ways that are both effective and generate respect with your people?

And here's the big one ...

> **You may be their manager, but do your people have a leader?**

This is the question we really need to ask ourselves ... and of course, how we might answer it isn't nearly as important as how our people might answer it ... and make no mistake, they answer it every day. Never forget, our people are constantly watching and evaluating us. Be the manager ... be the leader your people need.

PUNCH-OUT THOUGHTS:

In an earlier chapter we discussed how, as retailers, we are in the 'customer perception business.' Well, maybe as leaders, we should think of ourselves as being in the 'employee perception' business.

By that I mean, what we do and what we say is only relevant in regard to how others around us perceive those words and actions. And if our employees perceive us to be a poor leader, then, we're a poor leader. It's their perception, not ours, that counts.

Now I know that's a difficult philosophy to accept ... it was for me, too. But think of it this way ... if our job is to help our employees succeed ... if our purpose is to help them get better, and we're not able to do so, then we failed at what we're supposed to accomplish. And, if that's the case, how can we be an effective leader?

— Chapter 6 Notes —

- *So, do your people have a manager, a leader, or a good leader? Why do you feel this way?*

- *How do you think your people would answer that question? Would they all answer it the same way? Why or Why Not?*

- *What's one thing you could do today, that would start you on the path of becoming a good leader or enhancing the one you are?*

VII

DO I SPEND AS MUCH TIME PRAISING AS I DO CORRECTING?

PUNCH-IN IDEAS: In the retail industry we're taught to continually look for things that need to be 'corrected,' or brought up to standards. Before we open the doors each day, we 'walk the store' or our department making a final check and identifying any items that need to be corrected. We do the same thing before the big boss comes in, before we go home at night and at least two or three times a day. We become good at finding things that aren't right?

I jumped out of bed as my alarm went off at 5:30 AM. We were out of English Muffins, so I got in my car and hurried down to my local supermarket. As I pulled up I noticed one of the assistant managers out rounding up some carts that were left in the lot during the night's business. I could tell it was the assistant manager because he had a real nice shirt on and looked the typical assistant manager part. I smiled as I remembered how many times in my life I'd done the cart round-up routine.

Since this store is open 24/7, I wasn't worried about gaining entry, but as I walked in I could immediately see it was still set for the night business. Only one of the two entry doors was unlocked ... the frozen food cases and most of the refrigerated cases still had their lights off ... the aisles I looked down seemed blocked and stocked ... a few DSD delivery people were putting the finishing touches on their display areas ... and a handful of employees were hustling around trying to get everything else in order. For anyone that's worked retail you'll know what I mean when I say there was a good feeling in the air, almost an anticipation, as everything was coming together for a new day of business. This was always one of my favorite times at retail ... a time when everything was looking good and ready for another big day of business.

I went down the bread aisle, and sure enough, the bread vendors had already been there and the aisle looked real good. I smiled again as I reached way in the back and pulled out a package of English muffins. Yeah, I know I should have taken one of the packages up front, but this is a habit I just can't break. I then re-arranged the two rows of English muffins so the display looked great again. But it was at this point that I noticed something.

Here came the assistant manager I had seen earlier but now he had one of his department heads with him and they were doing a walk thru down two of the aisles. It was obvious the department head was responsible for how these aisles looked and the assistant manager was following up and telling him the things that needed to be 'corrected.' Again, this was like a flash-back to my retail days both as the department head being told what needed to be corrected AND as the manager where I was doing the telling. Over the next few minutes I listened as the assistant manager walked down two aisles and continued his oration on the things that needed to be changed ... more stock here ... let's get this blocked a little better over there ... let's make sure the floor is clean here ... we're missing a sign on this display ... that end-cap display is sticking out too far, it needs to be pulled back in ... and on and on.

> *"Business is a lot like playing tennis ... the company that serves well rarely loses"*
> — Unknown —

Again, I laughed a little to myself, started to walk to the check stands up front and noticed the bakery manager and assistant going through the same routine in the bakery department and up front by the checkout stands, the Starbuck's manager was doing the same thing with one of her employees. I thought, "Man, some things never change ... that same stuff was going on in the late 60's when I started as a part-timer. The only difference is this manager is holding a computer where mine used to just carry a clip board. Besides that, it's all the same. Isn't the retail business great?"

Later in the morning after enjoying an English Muffin with coffee (the English Muffin was delicious by the way) I thought back over my morning run to the store and that's when it dawned on me ...

> **... not once did I hear a manager praise or compliment the assistant while conducting the walk-thru.**

Not once did I hear a mention of something that was done right or done exceptionally well. Not once did I hear a positive remark or comment about something that pleased the manager. Instead, all I heard were a list of points that needed to be corrected,

Of course, this shouldn't have surprised me because the retail world is an extremely fast-paced world and at the end of each day we only have a limited amount of time to get our stores back up to standards. So we've been taught to take a subordinate, walk the store and look for things that need to be 'corrected' before we open the doors or before the big morning rush starts or before our boss comes in, etc. "

As far as we know, this is an important part of being a manager. My manager trained me how to do it ... and his manager trained him ... and his manager trained him ... and well, that's probably the way it's been done all the way back to Ugg the caveman, the very first retailer. But I still found myself wondering, is this the best way to get these things done?

Okay, back to reality. This early morning English Muffin trip occurred over ten years ago and at the time, it really got me thinking about how we deal with our people. In short, as I came up through the retail ranks, praise was not a common occurrence ... at least it wasn't as far as I was concerned ... but being corrected sure was. Does this mean I didn't deserve praise, or there was nothing to praise me about? No, I don't think so. I believe it only meant that's the way the industry operated, and we just didn't know any better.

So here's my point, today we all know that praising someone for something they did right helps build confidence, morale, and repeat performance. How do we know these things? Well ...

- ... according to Gallup's research: "Employees who report they're not adequately recognized at work are three times more likely to say that they'll quit in the next year."
- ... biologists tell us that praise causes the release of Dopamine in the brain. Dopamine is a chemical that creates feelings of pride and pleasure.
- ... social scientists tell us very few people get much praise at work even though there are solid business benefits. Gallup studied over five million workers and concluded that those benefits include lower turnover and higher productivity.

But even with all of this information, as retailers, we were never taught to praise people. And based on what I saw during that early morning run to the supermarket, and what I've continued to see over the last ten years, it's something that still isn't being taught today. But if from nothing more than a personal reason, this needs to change ... and here's why. Once we become a manager ...

"... our success depends more on what our people do, than on what we do."

We discussed this earlier, and it's most definitely true ... as an employee, we're judged by what we can accomplish, but as a manager we're judged by what our people collectively are able to do. Therefore, if it's nothing more than from a selfish perspective, it makes sense to look for ways to get the best results from our people ... the best way to help them improve. So, do we get better results by continually correcting what are people do or do we get better results by praising people on the good things they do, and then demonstrating why other things need to be changed?

Well, most of us at retail are taught to correct people for the things they don't do instead of praising people for the good things they actually do. We're not taught to be leaders, we're taught to be managers. Not sure? I recently saw a definition of manager and leader that went something like this ...

... a manager tells people what to do, while a leader inspires them to do it.

Oh yes, I can hear some of you right now saying, *"I don't have time to inspire people, I've got a lot of things to get done."* And you know what? You're right, and I would have said the exact same thing. But do you know why we feel this way? We feel this way because that's the way we were taught, and that's the way we came through the system. But that doesn't mean it's the only way or even the right way.

This is one of the biggest awakenings I see happening with so many of the companies I work with today. It's a change in thinking ... it's a change in perspective ... it's a change in how we act and deal with our people ... but it makes a HUGE difference. All people want to believe they can succeed ... they want to believe they will be successful. And this is never more true than the people who work at store-level retail.

Our people want to believe they are appreciated and can be successful at what they do ... they want to believe they can advance. As a leader then, part of our job is to give them that hope, inspire them to try and then help them make it all come true. That's truly what a few of my bosses, later in my career, did for me and what I tried to do for my employees. And that's what we all should be doing for our employees today. I look at it as ...

> **"Do right by those that do right."**

As leaders, we should be paying attention and recognizing those people who are doing the good things. We should be doing right by those who are doing right. In fact, it's almost as if we have a moral obligation to do right and acknowledge and thank the team members who meet or exceed our expectations.

Plus, if we don't do right and thank them, can we expect them to continue to do right long term? Doesn't this saying also imply ... if we don't do right by those that do right, then we can't complain if they stop doing right? In other words, if a person does right for a long period of time, and no one seems to notice or recognize the effort being expended in order to do right ... then it's highly possible that person will stop doing right. Think About it!

— Chapter 7 Notes —

PUNCH-OUT THOUGHTS:

Okay, so let's make it personal and rate ourselves. Think back over the last few months and try to estimate the number of times we've actually praised someone for doing something right versus the times we've had to correct people for things they've been doing wrong. Are we more of a positive praise type of leader or a negative here's-what-you-did-wrong manager? Really take the time to review this ... and then decide if this is the way you want to be?

I would also ask that you take it one step further, make it more personal, and apply the same logic in looking at how you deal with your loved ones. You see, whether we're interacting with people as employees, people as customers or people as loved ones ... isn't it all the same? Isn't it still about how we provide input to help them?

So do you spend more time correcting their faults or praising their accomplishments?

Do you spend more time telling them what they did wrong or complimenting them on what they did right?

Again, is this the way you want to be?

Only you can answer that, but here are some additional questions to consider ...

- *What am I doing to help create a culture, both at work and at home, where we look for the good things people do and then praise them for it?*

- *Have I developed the habit of articulating specific actions that deserve praise?*

- *How do I provide effective recognition as a part of my leadership skills?*

- *When it comes to my spouse and kids, do I look for things to praise or am I more of a 'you need to do this' person?*

This week, why not really concentrate on looking for the good things people around you do? As you walk your store or department, or as you walk into your home, make a conscience effort to look for the good things people are accomplishing. I think you'll be pleasantly surprised.

As a leader committed to increasing our level of customer service, doesn't it make sense to at least ...

... spend as much time praising people as we do correcting them?

VIII

IS IT MORE IMPORTANT TO BE RIGHT OR DO RIGHT?

PUNCH-IN IDEAS: Everyone knows not to tell a customer, "You're Wrong" or "You Made a Mistake," ... but there are many subtle ways we do this every day. And by just paying attention when out and about, it amazes me how many examples you'll see of poor attitudes, laziness and just bad customer service. Everyone expects great customer service, but few people give it.

Recently, on my way to work one morning, I stopped by my local McDonald's to get some coffee. As I pulled up I noticed the drive-thru line was fairly long, so I decided to park my car and go inside.

As I approached the counter, a young man smiled at the customer in front of me, greeted him and said, "Hi, welcome to McDonald's, may I take your order?" The customer took a few seconds and then replied, "Sure, I'd like a large Coke and a Sausage McMuffin."

I watched the clerk punch in the order, print out the ticket, place it on the serving tray and proceed to get his food. When he came back to the counter he placed the breakfast sandwich on the tray. The customer looked at the sandwich and said, "Excuse me, this is a Sausage Biscuit and I wanted a Sausage McMuffin."

Now, I was expecting the clerk to make some kind of statement like, "Oh, I'm sorry, let me get you that Sausage McMuffin," but instead he looked at the customer and replied, "So you don't want what you ordered?"

Now I was surprised, and kind of shocked, so I can only assume the customer was too. He hesitated a moment then replied rather sheepishly, "Well, I thought I did order a Sausage McMuffin."

The clerk responded right back, "No, you didn't, you ordered the biscuit." Then he picked the Sausage Biscuit up from the tray, threw it into the garbage bin underneath the counter and called to the guys in the back to get him a Sausage McMuffin. I turned and looked at the lady in line next to me who had also heard the exchange. She just smiled and shrugged her shoulders.

The clerk returned a few seconds later, placed the Sausage McMuffin on the tray. I honestly don't know if he said, "Thank you" or not but I watched the customer pick up the food and go to a booth to eat. Nothing else was said, but I didn't want any problems so I made sure I didn't order a Sausage McMuffin and Large Coke. I can't remember what I did order, but after I got my food and sat down, I started thinking about that whole transaction.

First, I'm sure the clerk believed the customer ordered a Sausage Biscuit. Second, I would also guess when the customer said, "I thought I did order the Sausage McMuffin," the clerk felt as if the customer was accusing him of making the mistake. So, in response, he wanted to make sure the customer knew the mistake was his, not the clerk's.

Now truthfully, I thought the customer actually ordered a Sausage McMuffin, not a Sausage Biscuit ... at least, that's what I thought I heard. But as I watched all of this take place it suddenly occurred to me, it really doesn't matter who ordered what. It isn't about that! That isn't the issue!

And as I looked back over this entire scenario, three important points immediately jumped to mind —

First: for some reason, this McDonald's employee felt it was important for him to point out that HE didn't make the mistake. We don't know why he felt this way, maybe he was having a bad day, maybe he had just been reprimanded by his boss, maybe he had a fight with his girl friend ... we'll never know, but for some reason this employee felt it was important to make sure everyone knew.

Of course, from the customer's perspective, he didn't care who made the mistake, he just wanted his food.

Second: no matter what either of them could have said, both believed they were correct: the clerk believed the customer ordered the Biscuit, the customer believed he ordered the McMuffin.

Third: and this is the most important point ... it really doesn't make any difference, who did or didn't order a biscuit or a McMuffin. This should never have been about WHO made the mistake ... it should only be about making the mistake right. PERIOD!

Here's a question — If we went back and pulled the video tape of that transaction, and we could positively prove the customer had actually ordered the wrong item, would that one fact justify the employee's comments?

What do you think? Not sure? Well, ask yourself this, "Would proving the customer made a mistake improve the relationship between McDonald's and that customer? I mean, after being proved wrong, right there in front of everyone in the restaurant, would the customer feel better about the McDonald's corporation? You see, that's the problem ... in these situations ...

... it's never about WHO's right and who's wrong, it's only about what we need to DO to make it right.

The fact is, the customer may not always be right, but the customer is always the customer. And since they are the customer, our job is to make them feel good about their experience in our store, ... unless, of course, we want to lose them as a customer.

So for the 99.9% of our customers we want to keep, accusing them of making a mistake is NOT a good way to do that ... it doesn't solve anything because it doesn't make them feel good about their store experience.

In our McDonald's story, the employee lost focus on making the situation right, which would have been very easy to do. And instead, he tried to convince the customer he had ordered the wrong food item. But in doing this, he didn't make it right ... he didn't defuse the situation ... in fact, he actually escalated it. And, it could have gotten much worse.

Now, this kind of thing happens much more often than we realize. The point, though, is that it usually isn't as blatant as this. All it takes is an employee losing focus and becoming more intent on proving a point than satisfying a customer.

For example, it happens every time an employee tells a customer ...
- it was right there on the menu, didn't you see it?
- the sign was on the display, didn't you read it?
- you should have done it this way instead of ...
- you must have given us the wrong phone number
- you didn't follow the rules
- you really should have known better
- didn't you read the instructions
- why didn't you bring it back sooner
- you need to calm down
- well, it's our policy to .....

If you think about it for a minute, you'll see that each one of these cases is a situation where we're actually telling a customer "you're wrong." Oh, we don't say it quite that direct or in-your-face, but make no mistake, we're telling them that anyway. But isn't there a better way to handle these situations? Isn't there a better way to take care of incidents like these? So what's the solution? Well, here are four actions that may help.

1. CUSTOMER SATISFACTION IS #1:
First, let's make sure all employees know our #1 goal is satisfying the customer. Yes! Yes! I know you've told them that before, and I know they all understand it. But I've always found it amazing that we live in a country where everyone says they understand and know the importance of good customer service, plus they all say they want good customer service, yet how few people actually give it. So what can you do in the next few days to make an impression on your people about the importance of good customer service?

2. DON'T FEAR MISTAKES:
Look, mistakes are going to happen, it's part of business. We can reduce them, but there's no way to eliminate them. Customers make mistakes, employees make mistakes, managers make mistakes, ... and yes, even we make mistakes. Our employees need to understand there's no disgrace in making them. Just learn from them and move on.

3. NEVER ACCUSE A CUSTOMER:
We should NEVER, EVER accuse a customer of making a mistake. It's just that simple. There is absolutely nothing to be gained by accusing a customer.

4. IMMEDIATELY CORRECT THE PROBLEM:

A simple statement like, *"Oh, I'm sorry, let me get you that Sausage McMuffin,"* is not an admission of guilt. It's only a statement that we're sorry a mistake has been made, and we're going to make it right. That's all the customer really wants anyway.

As retail managers, it's easy to get caught up in doing so much manual work that we don't have time to actually manage. Here are three management points we need our employees to understand. As managers and leaders, these areas, and the subsequent actions we take, can actually improve our people, our operation and ourselves. Take your time, and think about what you can do to improve each of these situations.

• UNDERSTANDING GUIDELINES
It's important our employees understand what they CAN and CAN'T do to correct a customer's problem. What's one thing you can do this week to make sure they understand your company's guidelines.

• DON'T WORRY ABOUT MISTAKES
When our employees make a mistake, we don't want them to FEAR telling us. What's something you can do to impress upon your employees that you understand mistakes happen, and you just want to get them corrected and move on.

• SUBTLE WAYS
There are many subtle ways in which we can be telling a customer, "You're wrong." What idea do you have to help your employees understand this situation?

BE RIGHT OR DO RIGHT / 63

SPECIAL FOLLOW-UP: — While writing this chapter two events happened which I really need to mention.

EVENT ONE: Once I finished this chapter, I took a copy to a restaurant owner who is a good friend of mine. We had lunch together at his restaurant, he read the piece then commented, *"I certainly agree with everything you say, but we don't have that problem here, all of our staff are extremely customer service oriented."*

We talked a little more then he had to excuse himself to handle some duties in the kitchen area. As I was preparing to leave I overheard a discussion going on at the table next to me between a waitress and a customer.

It seemed the customer wanted to return her meal and order something else because the entrée she received had mushrooms in it and she couldn't eat mushrooms. That was when I overheard the waitress make the following comment, *"Well, it was right on the menu that this item had mushrooms in it. You should have known."*

That's when I immediately thought back to my friend's comment, *"we don't have that problem here, all of our staff are extremely customer service oriented,"* and I started to smile because here was a perfect example of the problem ... and it happened right after we discussed the issue. You see, everyone knows we should give good customer service, it's just that not all of us are (1) completely aware of exactly what all that means ... and (2) no matter how good we think we are, we still slip up every now and then.

EVENT TWO: I was in contact with a printing company and had left my phone number and email address for them to contact me. Later in the day I received an email saying they had been trying to reach me by phone, but they must have "written the number down wrong because the number they kept dialing was out of service."

After I read the email I went and looked at the original contact information I had sent them. That's when I realized I had given them the wrong area code, ... the mistake was mine not there's. I started laughing because this again was the exact point of this chapter. The individual at the printing company could have said, "**YOU** must have given us the wrong number" or "the two of us must have miscommunicated" or "did **YOU** give us the wrong number?" ... but instead, she said, "**WE** must have written down the wrong number."

They didn't care who had made the mistake ... they didn't accuse me of making the mistake ... they just wanted to correct the situation and move forward. This is the whole point of this chapter.

> **So how would your people have handled this particular situation? Do you really know?**

— Chapter 8 Notes —

PUNCH-OUT THOUGHTS:

- *What can you do to remind your employees that satisfying customers is their number ONE goal? How else can you Print It? Display It? Say It?*

- *How can you demonstrate to your employees that they should never, ever accuse a customer of making a mistake? Yes, I'm sure they'll say they never would ... but is there a way to show them how many subtle ways this could be happening right now?*

- *How do you react when your employees make a mistake? Can they count on you to help them correct it? Do they fear telling you? What can you do to improve this?*

- *Do your employees know the guidelines they can use to correct a mistake? What are they allowed and not allowed to do? When was the last time you discussed these guidelines with them?*

IX

WHY DO YOU THINK YOU'D BE A GOOD FIT FOR OUR COMPANY?

PUNCH-IN IDEAS: For most retail managers hiring people is almost like a necessary interruption from our daily work ... "okay, I've got to find another person to work the afternoon shift, let's get a person hired, then I'll spend some time with them to see if they'll work out." We view it as two different functions, 'get a body hired' and 'then we'll see if they'll do.' Even though we don't have much time to interview applicants, there's got to be a better way.

Do you remember the first time you actually conducted a job interview? No, not the first time you interviewed for a job, but the first time you actually interviewed a person for a job in your store or department? How did you do? Were you nervous and unsure about what you should say or do? How about your final decision ... was it a good one? Did the person perform the way you thought they would?

Research shows that one of the most difficult functions for a new retail manager is hiring people. And, selecting the wrong people always ends up costing us time and money. That's why making good hiring decisions is an important first step in building a solid retail operation. Based on my experience, this is caused because retail managers receive very little training for, or support during, the hiring process.

> *"You're only as good as the people you hire."*
> — Ray Kroc —
> McDonald's Founder

I remember the first interview I did. Oh, I knew the basics like: introduce myself ... give the person my undivided attention ... make sure I explained the job and salary ... answer their questions, etc. But as I sat down later in the week to make a decision, I realized I really didn't know much about the people I'd interviewed at all ... just the name, rank and serial number kind of information. So what did I do? I made my hiring decision the way most of us do ... on gut instinct.

In fact, as I think back during those first years as a manager, most of my hiring decisions were based on two things and two things only .... how quickly I could get a body hired and into my department AND my gut instinct.

Yes, I made some good hiring decisions and I made some poor ones ... and, yes, I knew there had to be a better way, but to tell the truth ..... I just didn't have time to go through 10 interviews, 30 minutes each, over a three to four day period, with long drawn out conversations about this and that. This was retail, and if I needed to get someone hired, I needed to get them up and going as fast as I could. So yes, gut instinct became my primary hiring qualification.

Then years later I met the head of one of the largest retail companies in the United States. We were talking about our experiences coming up through our different companies when he commented that one of the most important points he learned was "to hire the attitude, then train the skills." I asked him what he meant and he responded, "I found I could always improve a person's skills ... almost anyone can learn how to do a certain task or a particular job ... but I always had a difficult time trying to change a person's attitude."

"The closest to perfection a person ever becomes is when they fill out a job application form."
— Stanley J. Randall —

As I quickly thought back on the people I had hired over the previous years it dawned on me that the difference between the good hires and the poor ones usually came down to that person's attitude. I also realized that was exactly what I was trying to determine by using my gut instinct ... I was trying to determine a person's attitude and how well they'd fit into the department.

We talked a little more about how to determine a person's attitude and he gave me a few easy things to try. Ever since then I've used them over and over with great results. I'll show you those later in this chapter.

Once I switched to hiring people based on their attitude, instead of any skills they said they had or grabbing the first person I saw because I needed a body, everything seemed to change. My hiring decisions got much better, I had less turnover, and everything seemed to get much easier.

I guess I shouldn't have been surprised. Don't we all prefer to work with people with whom we get along? And wouldn't we all rather work in a place where everyone pulls together to get the job done ... a place where people are positive and upbeat about their work? And, more than anything else, doesn't this all come down to a person's ATTITUDE?

The point is, one of our most important responsibilities as a manager, is hiring people. Remember, we're responsible for what our employees do and what they accomplish. So when it's time to hire a new person, we need to do everything we can to make sure that person will perform at, or above, the level we need. The new hire will be a direct reflection on us and we should look at the hiring opportunity as a chance to add a top draft choice to our team. Our success depends on it.

I guess I had never thought of it that way before. But once I learned how to quickly get a feel for a person's attitude, my confidence in hiring the right people improved and I made much better hiring decisions.

Here are the four areas my business friend explained to me. They've become the basis for every hiring decision I now make! See what you think.

I. INITIAL IMPRESSION

The minute you meet the applicant, ask yourself two questions:

A. *"If I were a customer, would I want to be served by this person?"* This initial "gut response" is important because your customers have gut reactions, also.

B. *"How does the applicant look?"* If an applicant isn't willing to clean up and present themselves in a well-prepared manner for the interview, how can you expect them to do so for your customers?

Sections II & III are where we try to identify a person's ATTITUDE. We use a system officially referred to as "Behavioral Interviewing Techniques." This means we ask questions which require the applicant to respond about how they act in certain circumstances. Carefully read these next two segments, and see if any of the examples can help you improve your interviewing skills.

II. WHO THEY ARE AND HOW DO THEY ACT

Here we ask questions that require the applicant to demonstrate how they behave during certain situations. *(I actually wrote these questions on my interview sheet so I wouldn't forget to ask them and so I could write down any important responses.)* Question examples include ...

- Customer service is very important in our store, give me an example of you delivering exceptional customer service?

- How did you handle a difficult customer situation?
- If you get this job, describe the kinds of things you will do to provide superior customer service.

It's amazing, but I've found by asking these types of questions, then listening to the responses, I can gain a fairly accurate picture of the applicant's ATTITUDE toward customer service.

In fact, their **ATTITUDE toward the question** and how they **represent themselves while answering it**, will usually be more important than the actual answer they provide. Pay attention. It's amazing what you'll be able to learn.

I also use this same type of question to help determine an applicant's ATTITUDE toward other workers, their bosses, work schedules, etc. Try a few examples like ...
- Give me an example of how you handled a situation when you weren't happy with that week's work schedule?
- Every once in a while we all find a person we just have difficulty working with. How do you handle those type of situations?
- Give me an example of how you handled a time when you knew you were going to be late for work?

Also, if an applicant is applying for his first job, these questions can still be used by adapting them to address behavior experiences at school or home.

III. PREVIOUS WORK HISTORY

Another "telling" ATTITUDE area is exploring the applicant's current work status with questions like ...
- I see you currently work at ABC company. What is it about the company that makes you want to leave?

- I see this would be your first job, what is it that causes you to now want to go to work?
- What is it about our company (or this job) that makes you think you would be a good fit?

Again, I ask the question, then shut up and listen to their response. And remember, it's not as much what they say as it is their ATTITUDE toward the question and how they represent themselves while answering it that counts. Pay attention.

IV. IDENTIFY ANY TECHNICAL SKILLS

And lastly, I'll usually check to see if the applicant has any technical skills that might help in this job ... if they've previously used a register, stocked shelves, ordered inventory, etc. I know I'm going to have to spend time training them anyway, but if they have previous experience with these things it might make it easier for them.

Two additional points to remember ...

(1) if you have a red flag go up during the interview process, nine times out of ten it went up for a reason. **Don't ignore that RED FLAG.** So often we ignore, dismiss or make excuses for the applicant when that flag goes up ... DON'T! The applicant will never look better, act better or appear to be better than they do during this interview. This is their best! So if you feel a red flag go up here, believe me, it will go up even higher later on. So **Don't Ignore The Red Flag!**

(2) yes, you may have a significant amount of time invested in recruiting and hiring someone. For me I can go through this process in about 15 to 20 minutes. If I interview four or five people for an opening, I've still spent 1 1/2 to 2 hours of time just interviewing and I don't have time to waste, but here's the point!

Most of us at retail view the hiring process as "I just need to get a body in here and I need it now." We don't have time to waste, we need to get someone in place, so we're just concerned with getting someone hired ... AND THEN we'll worry about if they can make it or not. I know that's the way I felt, and in many cases that's exactly what I did.

And yes, I used to hear the same old rhetoric about how hiring the wrong person costs me time and money. But when I needed someone, I needed them IMMEDIATELY, I didn't have time to fool around. I needed them now! But here's what I failed to take into consideration, ... and I sure wish I had been different ...

... as a manager, each one of my employees will have a role in determining my own personal success or failure. Therefore, if for no other reason than that, when I get the chance to add another employee to my team, shouldn't I do everything I can to make sure that person can perform at the level I need?

You see, this isn't about getting another "body," it's about improving our team. We need to look at every new person we bring on as a critical hire. As managers and leaders, when it comes to hiring people, we need to **MAKE IT PERSONAL** ... because it is. Always remember, we are responsible for helping our people succeed, and because of that our own personal success depends on it.

Now we all know there's no 100% guarantee any person we hire will work out, but by taking the time to ask the right questions and then paying attention to the responses, I was really able to drastically improve my hiring success rate. I know you can, too. My only regret was not starting it sooner.

— Chapter 9 Notes —

PUNCH-OUT THOUGHTS:
- *What things have you experienced as "red flags" during your interviews?*

- *Did you ignore them or listen to them? Why? What happened later?*

Remember, if you have a red flag go up during the interview process, nine times out of ten it went up for a reason. **Don't ignore it.** *Remember, the applicant will never look better, act better or appear to be better than they do during this interview. This is their best! So if you feel a red flag go up here, believe me, it will go up even higher later on.*

- *How much time do your invest in recruiting and hiring?*

It took me about 15 to 20 minutes to go through the process I discussed here. Of course, if I interviewed four or five people for an opening, I'd still spend 1 1/2 to 2 hours just interviewing and I didn't have time to waste. But here's my point ... because of what I talked about in this chapter ...

... I began to look at every new person I brought on as a critical hire.

- *Does this make sense to you?*

*As managers and leaders, when it comes to hiring people, we need to **MAKE IT PERSONAL** ... because it is. We're responsible for helping them succeed and because of that, our own personal success depends on it.*

We all know there's no 100% guarantee any person we hire will work out, but by taking the time to ask these questions and then paying attention to the responses, I was really able to improve my hiring success rate ... I know you can, also.

- *Do you have a hiring interview sheet you use when you're interviewing for an open position? If you don't please make one.*

- *If you have a form or sheet, can you add some of the questions we discussed here to it? How would you do that?*

- *What additional things can you do to make it easier to handle interviews?*

Note: Most companies have their own list of hiring "Do's and Don't's" for interviewing a job applicant. The points mentioned here conform to the national hiring practices, but if you think any of them conflict with your company's hiring requirements, contact your HR department to get clarification before including these guidelines in your hiring criteria.

"THINK ABOUT IT" VIDEO SCENES

Here are a few scenes from our "Think About It" video series. These are short (3-4 minutes) videos discussing the topics introduced in this book. Many are available for download or they can be sent directly to participants through our unique e-mail program.

A person has to choose to become a swamp drainer, it doesn't happen by accident and it's not for everyone. Solving problems, instead of just reacting to them, isn't an easy road to follow.

It doesn't make any difference if we feel we gave good service ... it's what our customers think that counts. The customer's perception is our own reality. Period!

You may be a manager, but do your people have a leader? Most of us at retail are taught to correct people for the things they don't do instead of praising people for the good things they actually do.

The customer may not always be right, but the customer is always the customer ... and that means they get treated accordingly.

Solve a problem and you create a loyal customer who will tell 10 to 16 others about your company. Fail to make customers happy and you've made enemies who will each tell an average of 28 people about their terrible experience.

... before we can become a swamp drainer, we must be a good alligator fighter. We have to be able to handle the day-to-day problems before we can start looking at the bigger picture.

Learn To Think

All of a sudden my store manager walked by and asked what I was doing. Embarrassed, I quickly said, "I'm thinking." Then I tried to explain about this training exercise and the concept of learning to think at a higher level.

What Is Your Main Job Tonight?

Are you a salesperson or an "order taker?" You know the kind ... they take an order, fill it, next customer ... take an order, fill it, next customer ... and on and on they go. They don't care enough about their customers to find out what problems they have ... they just take and fill orders.

Employee vs Manager Difference

Since all of the work was getting done, my crew just continued at their same pace and let me keep working as fast as I could go. In fact, I think a few of them actually slowed down some just to see how much harder and faster I could go.

Learn To Think

"Buck, you obviously don't understand, you're not paid to think, you're paid to do what you're told."

Hire The Attitude

As a manager, we're judged by how our people perform, so every time we hire someone, we've got the opportunity to add a top performer to our team. We need to make the most of it.

What Is Your Main Job Tonight?

We had so many tasks to do at night that we started to feel, "I wish these customers would leave me alone so I could get my work done." In other words, our job became the list of "tasks" we had to complete ... and "customers" became an interruption that made it harder for us to complete our job. Do you think if employees had this type of attitude, a customer might even be able to sense their frustration and impatience?

Employee vs Manager Difference

Once we become managers, our success stops being about what WE do ... and becomes more about what our EMPLOYEES do. This can be a scary reckoning, because it means much of our success or failure will depend on how well our people perform.

Employee vs Manager Difference

One day he's a regular employee, doing his own thing, then "POOF," the next he's the manager. So what does he do? Well, he got promoted because he was a hard working employee who could get a lot of work done, so now he becomes an even harder working manager trying to do even more.

Am I Paying You Right Now?

Any time she found an employee who was 'on the clock' and not doing a work task, she would immediately ask, "Am I Paying You Right Now?"

Employee vs Manager Difference

Then, a year or so down the line he gets promoted to a bigger volume store, and WHAM, he fails miserably because there's no way he can do all of the required work at this bigger location.

Purpose of Business

I'm sorry, the purpose of business is not just to make money. Yes, turning a profit is critical, but making money is only one function of business ... it is not its purpose. The purpose of any business is to help solve a particular problem.

As managers, much of our success depends on what our employees do and accomplish. So when it's time to hire a new person, we should do everything we can to make sure we hire a person who will perform at, or above, the level we need. Make it personal.

If a red flag goes up during the interview process, nine times out of ten it went up for a reason. Don't ignore that RED FLAG.

Ask the right questions and then be quiet and listen. In fact, the applicant's ATTITUDE toward the question and how they represent themselves while answering it, will usually be more important than the actual answer they provide. Pay attention. It's amazing what you'll be able to learn.

Is it possible, since so few retailers actually give good service, that this is a great way to differentiate ourselves from our competition? And better yet, a great way for YOU to set yourself apart from your competition? Plus, isn't this what we should be doing anyway?

The position you hold today is something you were appointed to by being good in the past. What you did and accomplished helped you get your title.

But, being a true leader is much different. "Leader" is a label that is EARNED through specific behaviors. It's based on what you do today, and what you will do tomorrow — not what's printed on your name tag.

AS A MANAGER, WHY SHOULD LEADERSHIP TRAINING BE IMPORTANT TO ME?

PUNCH-IN IDEAS: Much has been written about leadership and the need to become a better leader for our people. This is true whether you're a manager, supervisor, director or a top company executive. I think each one of us would like to be regarded as a good leader, but how do we start? And, is it possible to be a good manager and a good leader at the same time?

A few years ago I heard the quote: **"People quit their bosses long before they quit companies."** Usually I have to repeat a quote over a few times before the meaning comes through, but not with this one. I understood this quote immediately because it's something I've seen countless times. Basically it means, how we feel about our boss is much more important in deciding if we like or dislike our job and our company than the company rhetoric or culture. In other words, no matter what the company 'policy' may be, it's our bosses' actions that cause us to feel if our daily efforts are productive or unproductive ... appreciated or unappreciated ... fulfilling or a waste of time. No matter how wonderful our company might be in building and developing people ... if our particular boss is the exception to that rule, then we look to leave.

Do you agree? In my work I've found most people judge their company by how well they like their boss. They feel motivated, inspired or shackled and unappreciated by the particular relationship they have with their boss. If they like their boss, they like their company ... but if they don't like their boss, then watch out because they're looking to leave. Now that's fairly easy to understand, but I think it goes much deeper than that because this statement really demonstrates ...

> **... how we lead directly effects the satisfaction levels our people experience at work.**

Think about this for a minute. The more we, as managers, meet our employees' needs for attention, guidance, support, development, recognition, etc. – the less likely it is they'll start looking to find them elsewhere. Plus, the flip-side of that is equally valid ... the more we don't meet those needs, the greater the likelihood they'll start looking somewhere else to find them.

Don't you find that to be true? Think about your own situation, your own boss or the bosses you've had in the past. Isn't this the way you felt? And yes, we all understand that pay and money issues can also effect turnover, but research has shown over and over again that most of the time employees pull out their resumes because of <u>management problems</u> not <u>money problems</u> ... because of a lack of <u>management caring</u> not a <u>lack of compensation</u>. These are important points for us to understand.

First: the majority of people who leave a company do so because of management problems
and
Second, how we lead, directly effects how our people feel about management problems

Recently a somewhat misguided manager told me, "Nowadays, no one is going to walk away from a decent paying job." Well, based on what I'm seeing, that ain't necessarily so! Don't let a tough economy with high unemployment fool you into thinking that retention is no longer a business concern. Granted, in a tough economy fewer people are apt to quit but we still need to worry about the competition who would like to steal our best people and even more importantly, how about those folks who quit ... and stay!

COMPETITION STEALING OUR PEOPLE

No matter how challenging the job market may be, there will always be a handful of competitors out there who will be more than happy to steal our best workers. And, just as every customer is critical to our success, so are our best employees.

PEOPLE WHO QUIT AND STAY

We've all seen people like this. These are the folks who have already quit, in their mind, but their bodies keep showing up. These people drag down production numbers, customer service goals, even injury numbers because mentally, they've already left. They talk about how bad the company is ... how they hate working there ... how bad their boss is ... but they don't leave, they just hang on and on and on.

I learned this a long time ago, and it may be even more important now than it was back then ...

> ... employee retention is not about keeping BODIES,
> it's about keeping MINDS and HEARTS.

This is so important. I know as a retail manager there are times we just wish we had more bodies to help take care of particular problems, but the fact is, we not only need our people to show up, we need them to show up well. So the question we really need to ask becomes ...

... what can I, as a manager, do to capture my employees minds and hearts and become the leader I want to be?

As we've discussed in earlier chapters, making the transition from a manager to a leader doesn't happen overnight. The title 'manager' can be given to you, but you must earn the 'leader' label and it takes time. But you can begin that transition right now, by memorizing one little sentence ...

We manage 'things' but we lead 'people!'

I love this seven-word sentence. The very essence of managing and leading is spelled out in its simplicity. Obviously, we can't lead things like an order system, or a timetable, etc. ... we can only manage them. Hopefully we're good at managing these things.

In the same way, no matter how much we'd like, we can't manage people, we can only lead them. This is because our people are watching and they react to what we do, no matter if it's good or bad. Therefore, we need to remember, in ALL of our dealings with people, we're leading them. The question is only, do we do that well, or poorly?

> *"Effective leadership is the only competitive advantage that will endure. That's because leadership has two parts - what a person is (character) and what a person does (competence)."*
> — Steven Covey —

In the rest of this chapter we've outlined eight questions we should ask ourselves and answer, at least once a quarter. Plus, as we answer these questions we should construct an "Action Plan" we can use to rectify any shortcomings we might find. But right now, remember the "We manage things but we lead people!" quote and then read and think about each of these eight questions. Ask yourself ... Do I do these things? ... When was the last time I demonstrated this example? ... Do my people feel this way about me? Think about each of these questions and have some fun while going through each one.

Question 1: Am I Setting The Example I Want?

Our people constantly watch us to see what we're doing. They learn what's acceptable behavior — especially when it comes to ethics and integrity — by watching our actions. Regardless of what's said or written, our actions, whether good or bad, are the performance standards they will follow. So if we want to be a successful leader, ... we must set the example. We must be the first to 'walk our talk' and 'practice what we preach' when it comes to things like:
- following ALL of the rules and procedures
- treating EVERYONE with dignity and respect
- ALWAYS telling the truth
- NEVER breaking a promise or commitment
- building superior quality into EVERYTHING we do
- CONTINUALLY giving our best effort
- CONSISTENTLY taking a stand for what's right

So, are you trustworthy? Do you do what you say you're going to do ... ALL of the time? Are you accessible to your employees? Do your employees know how to reach you? Are you a role model for honesty, integrity and walking your talk?

Question 2: Am I CONSIDERATE of my employees' needs?

Our people want to know we're as interested in them, as people, as we are in the specific job or task we need them to do. Truthfully, we can't possibly focus on our mission without focusing on the people that make the mission happen. The two go hand-in-hand. Plus, since we manage 'things' and lead 'people,' common sense suggest that it's the people who are at the core of all leadership activities.

Do your employees think you care about them as people or do they believe you're only concerned about getting the job done? What have you done to demonstrate that you care? Do you ask them about their families? Do you know the names of their spouses and children? Are you responsive if they need time to handle certain personal problems? Do you demonstrate respect for your employees' time and talents ... as well as RESPECT for THEM as individuals?

Question 3: Do I provide employees with the training, tools, resources, and feedback they need in order for them to be successful?

One of the most frustrating points employees tell us in our workshop surveys is being given a job or a task to do, yet not given the necessary tools or support to get it done. This happens a lot more than most employers realize. Have you put employees in this position? The vast majority of employees want to do a good job, they want to be productive, they want to get better, so what are you doing to help them do that? Our job is to give them the opportunity to succeed ... it's to make sure they have the necessary tools, training and support to get the job done, and then the encouragement to try and keep going.

What have you done recently to help your employees get better, improve, move up the ladder? Do you know your employees' goals, their ambitions, their aspirations? If not, how can you help your employees achieve them?

Question 4: Do I keep employees in touch so they know "what's happening?"

No matter what the vision may be, we must communicate so all team members understand their roles and what each must do to achieve the vision. This makes everyone feel important ... it keeps everyone informed about what is going on in the company. This sounds like a simple point, but if you've ever worked for a boss that likes to keep facts to himself then you know how frustrating it can be. So be open, let everyone know what's going on.

What have you done to keep everyone in the information loop? Do you regularly meet with your employees, share what you know and update them on what's taking place within the company?

Question 5: Do I solicit and listen to, staff-member ideas and concerns?

One of the biggest opportunities for leaders is helping their people see they make a difference. People want to feel they are making a worthwhile contribution to the overall success of a particular project, group, or the company itself. They want to know they make a difference.

Research shows that people who do feel this way are much more loyal to the company, will continue to produce at an even higher level and make much more productive employees. Providing recognition and/or praise helps build our people and make them feel they're part of the team. We need to find ways to acknowledge and thank team members who meet or exceed our expectations. They need to understand the importance of what they do and how it contributes to the overall picture.

Do I welcome ideas that are NOT my own? Am I open to what others have to say without getting defensive? Are my employees willing to share their ideas - even if those ideas conflict with mine? What kind of system, if any, do we have in place that allows for this idea flow? Do I praise my employees more often than I find fault with what they do?

Question 6: Am I committed to help everyone develop and grow?

Remember the old adage, "Give people enough rope and they will hang themselves"? Well, I like to think of it this way, "Give people enough rope so they can improve themselves." By that I mean, we need to give our people the opportunity to manage projects so they learn and grow. That also means we can't so micro-manage the project that they lose that growth opportunity. We need to let them make the decisions. We help them, but we don't over manage the process. Yes, some mistakes will be made, but that's okay, especially if our people learn from them.

Do you delegate responsibility ... and the appropriate authority to get the job done? Do you give promising team members the opportunity to handle some big jobs and encourage them through the total process?

Question 7: Do I confront performance problems early?

Most of us are reluctant to address performance issues as soon as we should. Often we ignore the issue hoping it will go away, magically, on its own ... or we send out a memo to everyone restating a particular policy hoping the culprit will read it and stop causing the problem. Sometimes we just look for every excuse to avoid the confrontation and then as they continue to grow we finally call the individual in and unload on them.

The one overall point to remember is 'if we see the performance problem, others in the company also see it.' And yes, we'd like to believe the person will change, adapt, or get better without any confrontation, but rarely does that happen.

When we see a problem, and we start making excuses as to why we don't want to address it right away, we need to ask ourselves the following question,

"If this issue is so important, why am I waiting until later to say something about it?"

The truth is, we need to address these problems right away because if we don't we're actually saying, "Well, the problem isn't important enough to address right now, so I'll wait." Obviously, that's not the message we want to give to the culprit, as well as to the rest of our employees. We need to face difficult situations directly, make the tough call, and do what needs to be done. It's much easier to confront challenges with courage and deal with performance problems early and calmly — before they get big.

Question 8: Do I distribute the work and workload fairly?

As a manager we're responsible for writing the weekly schedule and for deciding who does what throughout the week. Do you schedule your employees fairly? Do you try to balance the responsibilities evenly throughout the day?

— Chapter 10 Notes —

PUNCH-OUT THOUGHTS:
Leading others can be a complex and challenging task full of good intentions which must be backed up with good leadership practices. Yes, it's important to ask and answer questions such as these throughout our management tenure ... but remember, the one truth about asking questions such as these is this ...

> *... how we answer these questions about ourselves isn't near as important as how our people would answer these questions about us.*

- *How do you think your people would answer these questions about you?*

- *Does that concern you, or is that something you'd like to know? Really be honest here!*

One area that's become extremely popular for companies we work with is to ask these questions not only of the manager, but also of the manager's employees. Then we compare the two sets of answers. That's where the reality hits the road. Yes, it's important how the manager answers these questions, but it's how the employee's answer them that's the real key. Remember, how employees feel about the manager is the reality of their working experience.

Don't forget, when we talk about customer service we point out that whether or not a person gives good customer service depends on how his customer feels not on how he feels. Well, isn't it the same thing here?

So whether or not you're a good leader or practice good leadership traits really depends on how your employees feel, not just on how you feel.

- *So how did you answer these questions? Are there areas you feel you should work on to improve?*

- *What kind of things can you do to improve in those specific areas? What action items would we find on your list?*

- *Even better, what things can you do right now to start that improvement?*

XI

IS THE CUSTOMER ALWAYS RIGHT?

PUNCH-IN IDEAS: This is a good question to ask a new hire or even a long term employee! If they answer 'yes' or 'no' just say, "Why?" and "Can you give me a few examples of what you mean?" Then just sit back, don't say a thing and listen. You'll learn a lot about how that person feels about customer service by watching their body language and listening not only to what they say, but how they say it. Pay attention! Now here's how I'd answer this question ... what about you?

Okay, here we go! Are you ready? Yes, I've wanted to say this for a long time, and I'm finally going to do it. Ready? Here goes! "The Customer is **NOT** Always Right!" There! I've said it! I'll even say it again, more slowly this time ... 'The ... Customer ... is ... **NOT** ... Always ... Right.' And look, the sky didn't fall, the earth didn't stop turning and no lightning bolt struck me down ... at least not yet. Of course, I do hear they're predicting a major storm this afternoon but ... nah ... that couldn't be about this.

Anyway, from as far back as I can remember, I've hated that 'Customer is Always Right' slogan because it was a lie. I knew it, my bosses knew it, and their bosses knew it, but that still didn't stop them from trying to drum it into me whenever they got the chance. For me though, the harder they tried, the sillier and more ridiculous the whole situation became.

I mean, come on, anyone that's actually worked at retail has had to deal with customers who were wrong by either demanding things, saying things or even trying to do things they shouldn't have. I kept thinking, at least be honest with me. There must be a better way to look at this whole customer interaction process so we can stop this 'the customer is always right' stuff? There just has to be a better way to explain it.

Then a few years ago, my wife and I were watching an episode of *"Everybody Loves Raymond."* I really liked this sit-com and it was the episode where Debra runs for President of the school's PTA. During an argument with Ray, Debra makes the following comment, *"it doesn't make any difference whether you think I'm right or wrong, I'm your wife and you're supposed to support me."*

Now, as it turned out, that one little innocent TV show comment led to a much broader, heated and a lot longer lasting discussion between my wife and myself ... of course, that's another story, and we don't have time to go into that here (it'd probably add another ten pages to this book). But that comment, and the ensuing discussion did make me think a little different about this "customer is always right' scenario. Follow me through this logic and see if you agree.

Let's start with this question, "Is your spouse always right?" No, come on now, I'm serious. Think about this for a minute and follow me through the concept. So, "Is your spouse always right?"

Well, as far as this discussion goes, I'll assume you, like me, didn't marry a Saint (even though they might try to convince us they are), ... so, I expect your answer is no ... no, our spouses are not always right. Okay then, even though they may not always be right, do you still support them? Are you there for them? Do you back them up if they need you?

Do you still try to help them? Now hopefully, your answer is, "Yes, ... sure I do!

But let's not stop there, in fact here's the next question. So even though we know our spouses may not always be right, why do we continue to support them? Why do we continue to try to help them? Why do we go the extra distance for them?

Now you may feel different than I do, but here's what I believe. We do these things because we have a relationship with them ... we care about them ... we want to make their life better ... and quite honestly, we don't want to lose them. And furthermore, because of that, don't we even set up a different set of rules of what we'll do and how we'll act for our spouse and for our family compared to the average person on the street?

For me personally, I've always tried to look at it this way ... "My wife may not always be right, but she's always my wife ... and my children may not always be right, but they're always my children." And because of that, I will treat my wife and children differently from all the rest. I will make more allowances .... I will support them longer and better ... and I will do whatever I can for them because of the relationship we have and how much I care for them. In fact, the truth is ...

... being right or wrong becomes irrelevant ... they're my family, and because of that I will act accordingly.

Now ... this is an important distinction for me because it focusses on **'who we are'** and **'what's important to us'** in the scenario, not on whether someone happens to be right or wrong. Also, and please understand, I am not saying our customers should be as important as our families ... at least not from a personal perspective, but what about from a business perspective?

Aren't customers our business' lifeblood? Doesn't our company's success depend directly on the customers we serve? Shouldn't a company have a relationship with its customers and care about them? So is it possible the same analogy we're discussing here could also apply, in some small way, to how a business should deal with its customers?

The more I've thought about this, the more convinced I've become we should do away with that old outdated "The Customer Is Always Right" slogan. It's embarrassing, degrading, and, as we all know, it's a lie. So let's throw it out, trash it! And instead, let's teach, embrace, and live this new one ...

> **"The Customer May Not Always Be Right, But The Customer Is Always The Customer."**

Now this is a statement I can understand, I can believe in. This statement's premise is simple, but it's true ... because no matter what, no matter how wrong we might think a customer might be, no matter what they might do, no matter how totally out-of-touch with reality they might appear ... they are still OUR customer. And as such, they receive special consideration, special attention, special patience, special care ... and they receive these things not because they are right or wrong, but because we desire a business-customer relationship with them, we care about them and want to help them.

For me, this is the true reality of the retail service business. I've spent more than 20 years working for retail companies, and another 20+ years working with them as a consultant ... and I'm convinced this is the one true fact on which everything else is built. And, if we can get our people to understand this basic premise, we can be extremely successful. It's just that simple. The customer may not always be right, but the customer is always the customer. PERIOD!

— Chapter 11 Notes —

PUNCH-OUT THOUGHTS:

When dealing with people we care about, whether they're right or wrong is irrelevant. What's important is we care about them, and as such, we treat them differently from everyone else.

- *If this is the reality of the retail service business, what can we do to teach it to our employees?*

- *How do we make sure our people understand and practice this concept in every customer interaction. Do we place that message on our back room walls? Do we write it on small cards and tape them to our registers? What can we do today, to start this transition?*

- *Is there a way to use this idea to set policy on how we should act and serve every person?*

- *Should we make sure every new person we hire understands this philosophy BEFORE they start working for us? If so, how do we get this done? What must be in place to make sure this happens?*

XII

I'M JUST AS GOOD, WHY DIDN'T I GET THAT JOB?

PUNCH-IN IDEAS: It's easy to get caught up in the old adage, "I'm just as good so why didn't I get the ... !" But plain and simple, being 'just as good' in anything is never enough. As I came up through the retail ranks I always knew that fact, but I never really understood all that it entails. I wish I had.

While growing up, I played a lot of sports and was fortunate enough to attend college on an athletic scholarship. I have worked, managed and coached in numerous youth sports programs and my oldest son coaches football on the high school level. I mentioned this because I've found many of the same motivation and leadership points I successfully used in sports, also apply in the business world.

This exact point was again brought to my attention when my son recently commented how during each year at least three or four parents will come into the office to talk about their son's "playing time." This includes everything from the belief their son isn't being given a chance to play, to he's not playing enough, or he's been put in the wrong position, etc. etc.

He commented, "Don't parents realize, as coaches, we want to win? Our jobs depend on it, and if we think their son can help the team win we'll do everything we can to make sure he's on the field. The real problem is parents don't seem to understand, it's up to their kids to convince us they are that good. It's their responsibility. And believe me, if they can show us, they'll play."

I thought about his comments quite a bit over the next few days, and I have to say, "I couldn't agree with him more." The truth of the matter is, it's up to the player (and no one else) to show he's good enough to be playing.

Ninety-nine percent of the coaches out there, want to win, and they'll play anyone they believe can help them win. It just makes sense then, if you are a player, and you want to play, it's your responsibility to convince the coaches that by playing you, they will have the best chance of winning. And this same philosophy applies for all levels of sport including high school, college and pro. But that's just half the story.

Sometime later I discussed this with my son and he added one more element that brought it to an even greater focus. He said, "Often parents say things like, 'my son is just as good, just as fast, or just as strong as so and so, therefore he should be playing just as much, too.'"

He continued, "What parents and players seem to forget is we're human, we can make mistakes. There are a lot of players out there, and we're not going to be able to watch all of them all of the time. But, the 'he's just as good as someone else' argument never works with me. I don't need someone to be 'just-as-good.' 'Just-as-good' doesn't make the team any better. 'Just-as-good' doesn't help us improve. 'Just-as-good' doesn't make us any more successful.

A player should never be talking about being just as good as someone else. They should be out to demonstrate they are better ... in fact, they are so much better that we MUST find a place to play them. In other words, they should be trying to take the decision away from us as to whether they play or not by being so motivated, so good, so hungry, so enthusiastic we have no choice but to play them."

Now again, I completely agree with this, and I've found the same philosophy applies to business as well as to sports. Think about it for a minute. Have you ever heard a colleague comment, *"I'm just as good as so and so, how come he got that promotion?"* or *"I've been here longer than ....!"* or *"I could do just as good a job as ...!"*

My point is this ... in business is being 'just as good as' Bob or Barb sufficient? Should being 'as-good-as' someone else constitute a worthy goal? Should we expect to move ahead and get that promotion or raise by being 'just-as-good-as' someone else?

Well, the answer is obviously, "NO!" No, being just-as-good-as doesn't give us the right for those things. But instead, why not take the decision out of your boss' hands by being so good, so extraordinary that basically there's no decision, it's automatic.

Now, let me get real here for a minute, take a step back and also let you know, there were times when I didn't feel this way. There were times and situations in my career when I didn't get the promotion I thought I should get, or I didn't get the raise I thought I deserved. And instead of looking at myself and what I could do to prove I was the best choice for the next opening, it was much easier for me to blame other people with the "I'm just as good as so and so" excuse. I even made some career choices at that time which really hurt me.

It wasn't until further down the line when I could look back and see what had taken place that I realized how misguided I had been. And because of that realization it really helped me turn things around. And it can do the same for you as well.

Doesn't it make sense that just as coaches want the best players on the field, business executives want the best candidates running their departments and stores? Why? Well remember, in both cases, coaches and business executives, their jobs depend on it. They need to be successful and they need the best candidates to make that happen.

Too many people like to blame other reasons when they don't get the promotion or the new job, just like parents blame the coaches when their sons don't as much playing time as they think they should ... but the truth, in both cases, is ninety-nine percent of the time ...

> **... we haven't demonstrated to our boss or coach that we are the clear choice.**

The point then, is to understand if we truly want something, our goal should be to prove to our boss and the surrounding culture that we, without a doubt, are the best possible solution. To accomplish this, there are three basic points we need to consider:

First, we need to look at the situation from our boss' viewpoint. What is important to him or her? What is he or she looking for? This is an important step because if we're focusing our efforts in an area that really isn't important to our boss, then we're wasting out time. So clarify your boss' priorities. Is it more sales, higher profits, increased growth, a well-run organization with less problems, better inventory control? What are the areas he or she wants taken care of the most?

Second, once we know those areas of importance, we need to concentrate on demonstrating we are, by far, the best choice to accomplish those things. That also means going beyond our defined jobs. If we are able to do more than is assigned or expected, we need to take the plunge and get it done. This is the best way to expand our horizons and increase our value as a team member and employee.

And third, we need to expand our area of notoriety and influence. We must find a way to engage others around us in our actions. This was the area that caused me the greatest problem. I just didn't get it! Maybe I was too young ... maybe I was just blind. But my perspective was, "I'm working hard ... I'm building a great operation ... I'm far exceeding my goals ... I'm ready for the next promotion."

Do you see the problem? It should jump right out and hit you. Yep, it's I'm ... I'm ... I'm ... I'm. It was all about what "I'm" doing. Now don't get me wrong I didn't talk this way and it wasn't all about me. I built a team of great people and we were accomplishing many wonderful things ... but what I didn't do was get outside my immediate departmental area. I didn't engage any of my peers or my boss' peers in our decisions or directions ... so as a result, no one outside our immediate group was part of the successes we experienced.

You see, I knew the 'none of us exist in a vacuum' idea ... I understood that basic principle. But what I didn't know was how to take it to the next level. Within a retail organization ... no one department exists in a vacuum ... no one store exists in a vacuum ... no one district exists in a vacuum ... they are all connected. An organization is a living breathing entity and we need to involve, include and engage people outside our immediate area (whatever that area might be: department, store, district, region, etc.) in our team as we move forward.

So the three keys become: determine what objectives are most important to your boss ... work to demonstrate that you're the best person to help accomplish those objectives ... involve others, outside your immediate area of influence, in attacking those objectives. Sound like a lot of work? Well, it's definitely more than the average person would do ... but then again, the average person is the one sitting on the sidelines saying, "Hey, I'm just as good. How come I didn't get that promotion."

Og Mandino, author of "*The Greatest Salesman In The World*," and past president of *Success Unlimited*, said it this way,...

> **"Deliver more than you're getting paid to do ... Make yourself so valuable in your work that eventually you will become indispensable. Exercise your privilege to go the extra mile, and enjoy all the rewards you receive."**

So work hard to leave no doubt ... work hard to leave no question. When you do, the answer then becomes obvious ... the answer becomes clear ... the answer becomes YOU.

— Chapter 12 Notes —

PUNCH-OUT THOUGHTS:
- *What extra-mile things are you doing right now?*

- *Are these things based on what's important to you or to your boss? Think about this because it's an important distinction.*

- *If you want to become indispensable, do you work on things you feel are important or on things your boss feels is important? Why?*

- *Who else is involved, outside your usual immediate team, to help with this project or idea? Have you contacted anyone just to get their opinion or viewpoint? Shouldn't you?*

XIII

WHY AM I UP TO MY NECK IN ALLIGATORS, WHEN I CAME TO DRAIN THE SWAMP?

PUNCH-IN IDEAS: Have you ever had one of those lives where it seems no matter how hard you work, you spend all your time putting out fires instead of truly getting anything done? Okay, maybe it wasn't your whole life, maybe it was just a year, or a couple of months. The point though, it makes no difference how long a time frame ... it's still a frustrating, unproductive helpless time.

It was my first day on the job with this new company. I had been hired to take over the deli operation and transform the departments into the newer prepared food versions seen around the country at that time. I spent most of my first morning being led from office to office, meeting the company executives ... and my last meeting, right before lunch, was with the Vice President of Merchandising.

We had the usual five-minute 'welcome to the company' talk. But as I was leaving his office, he stopped me and said, "Buck, just one more thing ... we're real happy to have you here, but many people are going to be pulling on you to get certain things done ... so I just want you to remember ...

... when you're up to your neck in alligators, it's hard to remember you came to drain the swamp."

I paused, laughed a little, thanked him, and said, "I won't forget" and walked out the door.

Well, as any new job can be ... the first couple of weeks were scary as I got used to the company routine and all I had to learn, but within a month or so I was rolling along. In fact, before the first quarter was over I felt I really had it under control. Yes, it got hectic at times, as I was also making weekly visits to each region, but I was working real hard and was keeping everything intact.

Then one night, after about six or seven months on the job, I was on my way home, tired from all the daily work grind, when it hit me. Here I was, running around trying to keep everything going and everyone happy, and yet I still hadn't accomplished what I was hired to do. Oh yes, we were moving things forward with our new deli operation, and things were better than when I first arrived, but I really hadn't done as much as I felt I should. I had let myself get sidetracked, I had let myself get pulled in so many different directions that I wasn't accomplishing what I had been brought there to accomplish.

> *"Success demands singleness of purpose."*
> — Vince Lombardi —

That's when my Merchandising V.P.'s comment came back to me ... "When you're up to your neck in alligators, it's hard to remember you came to drain the swamp."

Wow! I had only been there a couple of months and already I was fighting alligators. I wasn't quite sure if they were up to my neck yet, but they were coming at me from all directions, wanting my time and my attention. I also realized that many of the 'alligators' I was fighting would disappear if I could just drain the swamp. If I got the new ordering system done, for example, I wouldn't have the problems with shortages and overages ... I wouldn't have the constant delivery miscues ... or shrink issues because of excess product. It became very clear to me, I had swamps to drain.

I decided, right then that I had to make some changes, so I removed every non-essential task from my agenda and began to concentrate on my swamp-draining techniques. No, I didn't see as many salesmen each week, and no, I didn't travel as much as I had previously, but by the end-of-the-year, the departments and systems were completely transformed ... and sales and margins were rapidly increasing.

So, the main lesson I learned from my first year in management was ... if we let them, the daily tasks we think are so important and so necessary will expand to take all of our time, eventually robbing us of any opportunity to accomplish the bigger and more productive items. We can get so caught up in the day-to-day and even week-to-week alligator fights, that we forget to address the cause of the problems, the swamps.

And, yes, I know those day-to-day items are important, ... and yes, I know there's pressure to get them done, ... but I also know, as I found out later, the higher up you go in management, the bigger and deeper those swamps get ... the more alligators there are, and the larger, uglier and nastier they become. But no matter how big or deep a swamp may be, to be successful, we still have to find a way to drain it.

So as a manager, as a leader, why not make it a priority to learn to drain swamps now? Look around your operation and see if there isn't a swamp or two you should be working to drain. And one more thing ... every organization has a lot of alligator fighters, they're everywhere, and yes, some

"I am a slow walker ... but I never walk backwards"
— Abraham Lincoln —

are better than others ... but swamp drainers, people that can solve those big problems ... they're at a premium. So if you're looking to move up in your company ... become a good swamp drainer not just an alligator fighter!

So, what swamps are you supposed to be draining? When you were hired or promoted to manager, were there specific goals you wanted to accomplish? Are you satisfied with the progress you've made in those areas?

Are you being pulled in so many directions you feel you're just treading water, barely keeping your head above water while fighting one alligator after another ... or are you actually making things better by draining the swamp?

If we look across the business landscape we'll see thousands and thousands of retail managers working every day to handle their stores and their departments in all types of retail industries. And as anyone who's managed at the retail level knows, a big part of our responsibility is handling the never-ending barrage of problems and emergencies that are constantly thrown our way. In fact, in order to survive as a retail manager, it's almost imperative a person be a good 'alligator fighter' ... the nature of retail demands it.

> *"The secret of success is consistency of purpose."*
> — Benjamin Disraeli —

But as a manager, as a leader, we should also be committed to our own personal growth. We owe it to our employees, our company and to ourselves to keep growing and learning so we're a better manager tomorrow than we were today. Of course, there are many areas where we could improve, but one of the most important is becoming a 'swamp drainer' instead of just an 'alligator fighter.'

> **In other words, we need to search for ways to actually solve and ELIMINATE the causes of the problems and emergencies we deal with, instead of just REACTING to them.**

Sound difficult? Well, it's not easy, and no matter what we do, we aren't going to solve every issue, but making this change requires a different management philosophy.

You see, as managers, most of us just accept what's happening around us so we end up continually trying to put out the fires caused by all types of situations. This probably represents 90% or more of the retail management group. But why not move up to the higher management level, become more pro-active and actually look for ways to solve or improve the situations themselves.

A person has to choose to become a swamp drainer, it doesn't happen by accident and it's not for everyone. Solving problems, instead of just reacting to them, isn't an easy road to follow. But there are certain skills or traits that can point us in the right direction. Here are 5 key traits good Swamp Drainers possess.

A Swamp Drainer ...

• ... Is A Good Alligator Fighter

First and foremost, before we can become a swamp drainer, we must be a good alligator fighter. We can't just go off in another direction and let everything fall apart. We have to be able to handle the day-to-day problems before we can start looking at the bigger picture. It's just important to remember, that handling day-to-day problems doesn't solve the issue, it just buys us some time. How we use this time is the critical question.

• ... Is Willing To Look At The Bigger Picture

Often retail managers get so caught up in their own store or department, they can't see outside their own world. This is understandable because as retail managers we're focused on the store-level tasks we have to accomplish each and every day. But, if we truly want to solve problems affecting our operation, we have to willingly open up our viewpoint, take a much broader perspective and understand we're not alone ... there are many people (manufacturing, delivery, advertising, marketing) working to support our store-level efforts ... and we're all connected. And since we're all connected, one thing done in one area can have a major effect on results in another area. Understanding how it all works is the key here.

• ... Actively Searches For The Problem's "Cause"

We need to start conscientiously and consistently looking for the causes of the problems we encounter. The key is to start small and work on one issue at a time. See what you can do, within your own circle of influence to make one situation better. It may take making a call, talking with a peer, or any number of things. The key here is to start with a small problem then make the necessary adjustments to eliminate it.

• ... Sets Goals and Moves Steadily Toward Them

In order to attack these swamps, we need to set goals and stay focused on them continually moving toward a potential solution. If we don't, the day-to-day immediate problems will pull us back and we'll never get the bigger issues solved.

• ... Manages Their Time

In order to do these things, we need to be able to effectively manage our time.

Parkinson's Law states,
"Work expands to fill the time available for its completion."

In other words, "the amount of time it takes to do a specific task, expands to fill the time we allow for the task." We can't let this happen. We can't procrastinate. We have to learn to handle the day-to-day tasks efficiently and effectively so we have time to address the bigger issues.

Is there some new plan or idea you believe would really help your department/store but you just can't seem to find the time to pull it all together and make it happen? My suggestion would be to pay close attention and evaluate your effectiveness with the five areas listed above.

Note: The Merchandising Vice President I refer to in this chapter is Allen Noddle. I will always be grateful to him for his alligator story as well as being the individual who hired me and gave me my first corporate management opportunity many years ago.

— Chapter 13 Notes —

PUNCH-OUT THOUGHTS:
• One of the things we all have an equal amount of is TIME! We all have 24 hours a day, no more, no less.

Why then, can certain people accomplish so much more in their 24 hours than others?

Do you know? Why?

When I ask this question in seminars, I often get responses such as, "some people have more day-to-day responsibilities and less free time" or "time to do their own thing is a luxury for some people."

Maybe so, maybe so ... but according to Nielsen's March 2014 "Cross-Platform Report," ...

... the average American in the U.S. spends over 5 hours watching 'live' television and another half an hour on 'recorded' television every DAY!

Think about that ... that's over 2,000 hours a YEAR ... and that's not the average household, that's the average PERSON! Truthfully, do we have to go any further to understand why the average person in this country has some real 'time' issues?

- *No one says you have to go right out and try to drain the big swamps right away. In fact, as I mentioned earlier, I would recommend you don't. Over the years I've most often found, the bigger the problem, the more complicated and complex it can be. That's why it's better to start with the smaller issues and learn how to do these five things first. This gives you a chance to learn the techniques, develop some skills and gain some success before attacking those bigger more complex issues.*

- *What are some problems you have right now that you'd like to have solved? Think about this ... really come up with four or five.*

- *Okay, if you looked at your list, which one or two would seem to be the easier ones to solve? Why would you say that? What about them do you think makes them easier?*

- *IMPORTANT: The answers you just gave will help you identify where to start on solving those problems. Use your answers as your beginning point.*

XIV

WHAT CAN I DO TO INCREASE THE LEVEL OF CUSTOMER SERVICE WE'RE PROVIDING?

PUNCH-IN IDEAS: Since so few of today's retailers actually give good service, I'm beginning to wonder if we're becoming a society that's willing to accept mediocre customer service as long as it isn't 'too' bad.

The simple quotation, *"People expect good service, but few are willing to give it."* is attributed to Robert Gately, President & CEO, Campbell Corporation. His comment was made a few years ago in a discussion about the general lack of customer service in today's retail community. Do you agree with him? Better yet, how about this ..

... do you believe today's typical customer even expects good service?

I'm beginning to wonder because I'm not so sure. Maybe a better way to look at this is to ask yourself, "when you go out shopping do you 'expect' good service." Yes, I know we'd like to receive good service, ... and yes, I know we'd feel good about it if we got it ... but, my question is, do you really **expect** it?

Could it be possible, since so few retailers actually give good service, that we're becoming a society that's willing to accept mediocre service as long as it isn't 'too' bad? Two situations I see, almost make me believe this just might be the case.

1. — PRICE & SERVICE ARE LINKED

'Price' and 'service' have somehow become linked in a way where we believe we can't have both, a good price and good service. As an example: When we go into a low-priced discount store, we immediately accept the idea we won't receive a high service level. We even justify our feelings with thoughts like, *"I'm paying less for these items so I can't expect to get good service, too."* And then, when we don't get good service don't we justify that fact with other thoughts such as, *"I can't even find someone to help me, but the prices are so good I'll put up with it,"*?

The truth is, we've been conditioned to believe, as far as retail is concerned, "low price" translates into "less service" ... and the lower the price, the lower the level of service. We've been conditioned to regard it as a trade off! And conversely, don't we expect a higher level of service from the more expensive hotels, grocery stores, restaurants, department stores, etc.?

Over the last few decades the concept of "price" and "service" have become linked. We see ourselves as "paying" for good customer service, so we'll accept a lesser style of service in exchange for a lower retail price. That's one reason I believe many people really aren't expecting great service when they go shopping.

2 — FEW REALLY GIVE GOOD SERVICE

Another reason people don't expect good service is as Robert Gately says, *" ... few are willing to give it."* Oh, we often see and hear commercials, print ads, radio announcers and TV spots proudly declaring how a certain retailer is running "my kind of store," or that "my satisfaction is their only concern," or "customers come first." One of my personal favorites is the ad that declares "I'm Number 1." Wow, I didn't even know I was in the race, and now they're telling me I'm number 1.

Of course, more often than not, when we finally do get into their store we find a reality quite different from the fiction they promote. It's a shame, but the words we hear in the advertising aren't backed up by the actions we experience in their stores. Because of this, as a society, we rarely believe what we hear in an advertising message. Think about it ... do you really believe the ad that says they have the lowest prices in town or the one that says they give the best service? If you do I have some ocean front property in Arizona you might want to look at! I'll give it to you at the "lowest price" and I'll guarantee the "best service," too. Now isn't that a great deal?

Okay, so maybe fewer people are expecting good service, and maybe fewer retailers are actually providing it, but what does all of this mean? And what can we do about it? Here are a few points to consider.

First: We can't control what someone else does or doesn't do ... we can only control what we do.
This may sound simple, but it's really the way we need to look at this. We can't let how someone else or some other company acts effect how we will act. We have to stay focussed on what we want to be ... how we want to run our business ... and how we want to be remembered.

Second: If it's true that many people no longer really expect or receive good service when they shop, wouldn't that make it even more noticeable and appreciated if they did receive it?
In other words, at a time where less companies are providing great customer service, doesn't providing it become an excellent way to distinguish ourselves from the competition?

Think about yourself. Have you ever had someone, really go out of their way to provide you with great service ... service like they really cared ... service like you were really important to them? How did you feel about that service person? How did you feel about the company in general? Aren't these the same types of feelings we want for ourselves, our people and our company? Here's one more question,

> **"Did you contact the company or the person's boss to let them know how much you appreciated that level of service?"**

I'll come back to that point in just a minute. In the meantime, with a lack of great service providers, just think of all that could be accomplished if we truly committed (not just talked, but actually did it) to providing the best customer service in our particular retail category? How would we do it? What areas are the critical service areas for our customers? What can we do to solve and service those areas better than our competition, and better than other stores in our company? We don't have to wait for a corporate directive. What can we do right now, to start this "great customer service" ball rolling forward?

Third: Why don't employees give the kind of customer service we'd like to see?

What's wrong? I mean, we all "know" we should be providing good customer service. It's in every employee manual I've ever seen. It's written on the backwalls of store breakrooms and you'll even find reminders on cash registers across all retail formats. So what's wrong? What stops them from being those service oriented people we all would like to have taking care of us?

Well, my first point is, I don't think the majority of service people really understand what excellent customer service entails ... or what it's all about. There are so many subtle ways employees can help or hurt a customer service image ... and quite honestly, my research shows most entry-level minimum-wage front-line service employees have no idea what those are.

Also, think about this for a minute. If it's true that today less and less people are actually giving excellent customer service, then doesn't it naturally follow that (1) there's less opportunity for a person to actually see or experience it, and (2) as a newly hired employee, there's fewer role models to follow who actually provide it?

My second reason why I believe employees may not be giving the kind of service we'd like is very few people, including bosses, ever acknowledge when a person does give great customer service. When someone actually does go out of their way to really do a good job for another person, is that extra effort ever acknowledged? Do bosses recognize the increased service level? Again, based on our research, the answer to both of these questions seems to be, 'rarely, if ever.' And that's a major problem. Not too sure? Well then, just ask yourself, ...

When was the last time you, yes YOU, complimented or recognized one of your employees for giving great customer service?

No seriously, when was the last time? Come up with a date. How long ago was it? Do you remember when?

And here's the rough part ... the part we don't want to hear because it's the part we, as managers, must accept ...

> **... if our employees aren't giving the customer service we think they should, that's our fault, it's our problem, WE ARE RESPONSIBLE.**
>
> **But, if we have employees who at times do provide the level of service we think they should, and we're not complimenting or recognizing their efforts to do so, then WE ARE AT AN EVEN GREATER FAULT.**

This is one of the major problems we're seeing in today's retail industry and it cuts across so many different retail sectors. First, it seems fewer people are giving great customer service ... and second, even those that do are rarely recognized for doing so.

So a couple of year's ago I started living by the following motto ...

> **"I have no right to complain about someone's poor service unless I'm willing to acknowledge, compliment or praise someone else when they give excellent service."**

Does this make sense? Of course, this means when we see one of our people going out of their way to help a customer, we need to let them know we saw what they did and how much we appreciate it. That little bit of recognition can mean so much and help inspire that person to continue the increased level of customer service for others. Plus, this can also inspire other employees to do the same.

But that's just the beginning. In addition, whenever we feel ANY service person whether they're with our company or in a completely different retail sector, has gone the extra mile and provided us or someone we see with excellent service, we need to make it a point to personally tell their manager. This can be at a restaurant, grocery store, book store, or any retail operation. That's why I asked you earlier if you contacted the boss of the person who gave you good service? Wouldn't you want customers coming to you telling you how great they feel about the service your employees have provided? Shouldn't we then, do the same in return?

So ask yourself the following question ...

> **"What would happen if people actually started praising good customer service whenever they noticed it?"**

Instead of being lethargic about customer service, what if we really started recognizing it? What if everyone acted like 'secret shoppers' and praised the efforts of people who provided good service? Wouldn't this in turn, create more and more people giving better and better service? Yes, I believe it would.

Well, I'm not worried about saving the world right now, but I do know how important it is for us, as managers, to be more aware of how our own employees behave when servicing customers. We need to pay more attention ... be a little more watchful ... listen a little closer to what's being said. And not only should we be willing to correct someone who may fall short of our service standards, but we should be even more willing to compliment and recognize our employees when we see them go that extra mile.

And second, why not also pay more attention to those serving us in restaurants, stores, movie theaters, everywhere we go and then be willing to take the time to tell them and their manager, how much we appreciate their extra effort when they give it. Isn't that something we should be doing anyway?

> **In reality, maybe improving customer service is nothing more than each of us caring a little more about doing the right thing.**

Remember, what gets recognized gets reinforced ... and what gets reinforced gets repeated. Let's start doing right by those who do right! Think About It!

— Chapter 14 Notes —

PUNCH-OUT THOUGHTS:

- *Why would I, as a front-line retail counter employee continue to go out of my way to provide excellent customer service when, I'm not paid any more for doing it ... the other employees don't ... and my effort is never recognized? Come on, try to come up with a reason as to why I should?*

- *When was the last time you complimented an employee about going the "extra mile" for a customer? Think about it ... when was the last time?*

- *Here's another way to look at this specific issue ... how many times in the last month, have you complimented employees for going the 'extra mile?'*

- *Are your employees not going the "extra mile" or is it you just don't know?*

- *What can you do to pay more attention to your employees' customer interactions?*

XV

WHAT ELSE CAN I DO?

PUNCH-IN IDEAS: Do you want to be recognized for the unique person you really are? Most of us do, but that isn't necessarily the way it is as a youngster.

As kids, most of us want to be like everyone else. We don't want to be different ... we want to fit in ... we want to be accepted by our peers. In fact, being unique makes us different or odd, and that's a terrible thing for a kid to be. As we mature we begin to understand that just being part of the group, like everyone else, isn't always enough. We discover that as human beings, there's an inherent desire within each of us to be regarded as special in some way. We want to stand out, we want to be recognized for the unique person we are.

That's why just being normal, like everyone else, isn't natural. We're not made that way. We have this need to be special in some way, ... or better yet, to be recognized as extraordinary. Does this mean we need to become this highly motivated, success-driven, always on-the-go individual? No, not at all. But, as managers and leaders, it's important to recognize that each of us (employees, managers, supervisors and executives), have this need to be regarded as special, unique ... and even more important, it's how we fulfill that need that actually defines who we are.

> *"Normal is not something to aspire to, it's something to get away from."*
> — Jodie Foster —
> (actress, director, producer, who speaks three languages and graduated 'magna cum laude' from Yale.)

For me, this didn't happen until fifth grade. It was a special project where each of us had to prepare a report on one of the United States ... I got Maryland. I worked hard on the project but was still worried about the presentation I was going to have to make in front of the whole class.

On the Friday before my report was due, my dad came home, saw me working at the kitchen table and asked me how the report was going. I explained how I had gone to the library, gotten two books about Maryland, plus I had read the information in the encyclopedia and was now in the process of writing my report.

He then asked, *"Isn't that what most of the kids will do?"* And it was at that exact moment I knew I was in trouble.

Have you ever noticed that parents are experts at asking questions to which they already know the answers? And even worse, they make you give them an answer ... and you know, before the words ever leave your mouth, that the answer you're going to give them is not going to be acceptable?

My mind quickly raced over possible replies. I started to say, "No, Dad, most of the kids will probably only look at <u>one</u> library book, and I looked at <u>two</u>," but I quickly dismissed that one knowing it would just make matters worse. I began to sweat and could sense I was running out of time and I had to respond so I answered regrettably, "Yes, I guess so." *(I was hoping the "guess so" part would leave a little room for doubt which might save me but I really didn't give it much of a chance.)*

So there I sat, knowing what was coming. I could see it a mile away ... and yet it didn't make any difference because there was nothing I could do to avoid it. And yep, he didn't disappoint me when he asked, ... "Well then, what can you do to make your report different and better than the rest of the class?"

"Oh, no," I thought, "here we go. I'm almost done with this thing, and it's just an old report .... and now he's going to come up with more work I'll have to do. Or worse yet, he may think I should dress up in some type of Maryland colonial garb when I present this thing. What an embarrassment that would be."

I could feel the hours fly by as my dad looked at me waiting for an answer. I knew I had to come up with something or he would ... and that could be a even greater disaster.

At that particular time I had the encyclopedia open, and I was making a topography map of my state. He looked down and said, "Instead of just making the regular colored pencil topography map, why not make a real three-dimensional one?"

I didn't know what he meant, but I dared not interrupt and so he continued, "You could make a paste of salt, water and flour that could be molded into the shape of the state. Then you could add layers based on the topography levels and after it all dries, you could paint them different colors."

I still wasn't quite sure what he meant, but anything was better than having to dress up in some costume, so I was all for it.

As it turned out, my Dad and Mom showed me how to make the mixture and I worked to put the project together. I remember making the map, painting it and even finding a box that would hold the whole thing. But, most of all, I remember making my state presentation and then opening up the box and showing everyone the three-dimensional model of the state's topography. It really looked neat (much better than some of those colored-pencil maps) and I was as proud of that project as anything I had ever done.

The point I want to make though, ... I wasn't just proud my project looked good, ... I was proud that it was different, that it was unique, and that it was better than what other people had done. But more than that, I discovered something else that really surprised me, ... I discovered I liked that feeling. That's right ...

> **... I liked the feeling of doing something different than the rest. I liked the feeling of going further than what most of the other kids did.**

All of a sudden, just doing something like everyone else wasn't good enough any more.

From then on, that special feeling of creating something better, more unique, or different from everyone else drove me to look for ways to do special things ... and you can't imagine how many times I've thought back to the salt, water and flour map.

The point I'm trying to make here is not looking to be different for difference sake, that's not it. Instead, I believe in actively searching for ways to do something better ... to create a higher level of execution ... to be unique ... to be extraordinary ... and most of all, ...

> **... not to be willing to accept doing something "like everyone else" just to get it done.**

I believe the more we settle for 'normal,' the less extraordinary we become, but the more often we're willing to search for the extraordinary, to strive for a better way to do things, the more exceptional our life develops. So don't settle for normal, strive to be exceptional. That's a lesson my Dad taught me back in fifth grade. Oh, in case you wanted to know, I "aced" that fifth-grade state project.

So what about you? How have you fulfilled that need? What about the day you were promoted to manager or supervisor? Did you feel special? Did you feel unique? Maybe you even felt extraordinary.

What about the things you've accomplished up to this point? Have you constantly done things that made you feel this way or do you feel instead of being special, you're spending more time treading water, just trying to stay afloat? Well, welcome to normal, because I bet anyone, who's ever worked retail, has felt that way at one time or another.

But how can you change this? What can you do to become more extraordinary in your company, in your career, in your life? First, understand that being special and being extraordinary is not something you sit and wait for ... it is something that is there, right now, waiting for you. But, it won't come to you, you have to search for it, you have to go after it.

Second, here's a suggestion. This week, when you encounter a familiar plan and you want to make it better, more extraordinary, all you need do is ask one question ...

What Else Could I Do?

The truth is ... asking this question ... honestly, trying to answer it ... and then putting those answers into action can change your life.

So ask, **"What else could I do in how I ...**
- **... display my products?** What better methods can I use to get my items in front of my customers? Is there a way to display them which will engage potential customers on a higher level?
- **... ship my products?** What could I change to get my products to my customers faster?

- **... box or package my products for shipping** ... or in how they leave the store? Are my products protected when they leave the store? Is that important to my customers? If so, what can I do to improve that area?
- **... advertise my products?** What other venues could I try? What could I do to attract customers who may be walking or driving by? Once a customer is in my store, what can I do to make them more comfortable, or see and buy more products?
- **... market my products?** What groups or associations are in the area that could use my products?
- **... follow up after my products are delivered?** How could I contact customers to see if they liked the way we handled their business? Are there things we could do to improve?
- **... sell my products?** ... talk about my products? ... stock my products? ... help customers order my products?

This is just a beginning list of a few of the questions we could ask ... AND ... should be asking, but it doesn't stop there. From a personal point-of-view, what if we asked ... **"What else could I do to ...**

- continue to learn and grow?
- stay in better health?
- plan for my retirement?
- show my family/spouse that I love and care for them?

No, don't get worried. I'm not suggesting you ask yourself all of these questions at the same time. These are just examples of things to be considered. Also, you should realize, you won't always be able to come up with a workable answer. That's right, sometimes even YOU won't be able to find a way to make it better.

But, look at it this way. Let's say each week you pick a topic and honestly try to think of things you could try to improve that area. Let's say you can only come up with a real idea every other time. Let's also say that only half of your ideas actually work. That means, in a year's time, you've tried 26 ideas and only 13 of them worked. But, Wow! You've just implemented 13 new successful ideas in a year's time. Now I call that, **EXTRAORDINARY!**

The key here isn't how many of your ideas actually work, the key is to start building momentum ... start moving forward. You'll also find that as more and more of your ideas work, the easier it will be to develop new ones. You'll actually get good at this.

So if you really want to know how good it can feel to be moving forward, building a special life ... just take a 3x5 card (or the back of a business card) and write the following sentence:

> **What's one special thing I can do today that will make this an extraordinary day?**

Place the card on your bed-side table. Tomorrow morning, when you wake up, glance at the card and commit to one act you will do during the day that you normally wouldn't have done. Make this act something special for your company, your career, a friend, for you or for someone in your family. You choose. Commit to doing it and make sure you follow through!

Then, each night, as you get into bed, look at the card and think back on what you did that day and how it made you feel. Do this for seven days ... that's all, just one week, and you'll be amazed at how much progress you'll have made and how many extraordinary things you've been able to accomplish. You'll also be amazed at how good it will make you feel!

— Chapter 15 Notes —

PUNCH-OUT THOUGHTS:
- *At work, are there opportunities for you to do more, or better yet, do what you're currently doing only do it differently, better or more unique? Are you sure?*

- *What kind of things fall into that area? What opportunities do you see?*

So, what can you do today that no one expects you to do?

Examples you might want to try ...
- *develop some type of special promotional display for one of this week's ad items*

- *find some way of getting your employees and families together, outside the store, to build more team chemistry and unity*

- *start a special workout exercise routine you've wanted to try*

- *complete a task you've been putting off that needs to get done around the house*

- *go do that something special you wanted to do with your family*

- *plan a special romantic evening out with your spouse. Not just dinner ... make it extraordinary!*

The point is ... just get started ... move outside your comfort area ... do something different ... and you'll be amazed at how well you'll feel and how much you can accomplish.

XVI

AS A RETAILER, WHAT'S OUR PURPOSE? WHAT'S OUR JOB?

PUNCH-IN IDEAS: A few years ago a major business publication surveyed U.S. companies and found sixty-five to seventy percent of the executives in this country couldn't give a basic definition of what their job actually was. Oh, they could tell you what company they worked for, and their job title, but asking them to define exactly what their job was, left them cold. Surprising?

How would you answer the question, "What's your job?" Better yet, how do you think your employees would answer that question? In fact, if today you asked each one of your employees that question, what kind of responses would you get? Do you know? Do you think it's important to know?

Look at it this way. We are paying our employees a wage. They work for us. And we have certain expectations on the amount of work and on the standard of work that should be accomplished? Isn't it important then to know if our job definition and their job definition are the same, or even close?

In fact, if we really think about it, how is it possible to effectively manage a group of employees if we and our employees have different perceptions of what their job function actually is?

That's why I find this survey of top business executives so interesting ... according to their results, almost 3 out of every 4 execs couldn't give a basic definition of their job. Does that surprise you? Well then, in a sentence or two, exactly how would you define your job? Try it! See what you come up with. Hmm ... it's not as easy as it sounds, is it?

Maybe it would help to look at this situation from a different angle. What would you say is your job's main responsibility, what's your job's purpose? Is that easier to answer? Based on the way we look at jobs today, I'm not so sure. But I've always felt ...

> **... the purpose of a business is to help people solve problems.**

Okay, you must think I've lost it by now. Right? Well, when it comes to the purpose of a business, most people I know would say, "a business' purpose is to make money." Isn't that what's been drummed into us from the day we started at retail? Well, it may have been drummed into us, but I'm sorry, that's still not the purpose of business. Yes, turning a profit is critical, but making money is only one function of business ... but it is not its purpose. I still say, the purpose of any business is to help solve problems. Here's why I say that, and here's what I mean.

If I make clothing, for example, the purpose (my job) is to solve my customer's clothing problems. Maybe my customer wants a suit that fits better ... or one that makes him look more professional ... or one that is more comfortable ... or one that's easier to clean, etc. My job, my purpose, is NOT just to make a suit ... my purpose is to find out WHY he wants a suit and WHAT PROBLEMS he wants me to solve in making it. Doesn't that make sense?

Okay ... if I make writing instruments, the purpose (my job) is to solve my customer's writing problems by making a writing instrument that maybe makes it easier for him to write ... or one that is more stylish or fashionable ... or one that last longer or is more durable ... or one that writes so well it makes the message easier for others to read, etc.

> **The key in understanding a business' purpose is to look for the result of what the business' product or service produces, not just the product or service itself.**

Again, that's why a tailor's purpose isn't just to make suits ... it's to solve my clothing problem by making a suit that makes me look real good or fits a certain way or travels well or is very easy to clean, etc. Does that make sense?

So what about the retail service industry? For me, I started out working in a supermarket deli. I always believed my job (my purpose) was to help people solve their food problems. When customers came to the deli counter I viewed them as having problems ... it might be they weren't sure what they would get for their kids' school lunches; or the picnic they wanted to go on; or the party they were hosting that weekend; or tonight's dinner; or the card party scheduled for tomorrow night and on and on.

My job, my purpose, was to talk with a customer, find out what specific needs they had, and then use the knowledge I had about our products and services to offer solutions that would help them solve those specific problems.

Yes, I had to slice meat, scoop salad, prepare party trays, cook roast beef and many other things, but I always regarded these things as just <u>tasks</u> I had to do, ... but my job, my purpose was to help people solve their food needs.

Now, did everyone in my department feel that way? No. Some of our people were just "order takers." You've probably had some of those, too. You know the kind ... they take an order, fill it, next customer ... take an order, fill it, next customer ... and on and on.

So what's wrong with being an "order taker?" We'll discuss this topic in later writings but basically, order takers ...

- ... don't really care enough about the customer to want to help them, they just want to get to the next order. They see the task of taking and filling orders as their job.
- ... don't see the need to learn or educate themselves about the products they carry or the services they provide because they just fill orders, they don't help solve problems.
- ... don't create a difference, they create no uniqueness, they don't exceed customer expectations ... again, they just take and fill orders. From a customer's perspective, there is little or no difference between an "order-taker" at one store and an "order taker" in another ... both just fill orders, nothing else.

On the other hand, people who see their purpose as helping customers solve their food problems become more committed and engaged with the customer. They want to learn more about the products and services so they can offer better suggestions. They help create a unique environment, a difference, for the company and for themselves. This increases their job satisfaction as well as their value to the company.

Just look at the difference between these two jobs offered by the same company ...

JOB #1
In this job you will take the customer's order, fill it, then go to the next customer

JOB #2
In this job you will learn about all of the products and services we carry and be responsible for working with each customer to solve their particular needs. The more you learn and the more competent you become at this skill, the more valuable you become to us and our customers.

Plus, this same principal applies if you're helping customers solve their appearance problems at a dress or suit shop ... their shoe problems in a shoe store ... medical problems in a pharmacy ... lunch problems in a fast food restaurant ... reading needs at a book store and on and on. Think about it, businesses were developed and built because there was a need ... that need is really customers with a problem. Therefore, as sales personnel in business, our purpose is to help solve those needs, solve those problems.

The noted management expert, Jeffrey Gitomer said it this way...

> *"Isn't it really 'customer helping' rather than customer service? And wouldn't we deliver better service if we thought of it that way?"*

Isn't this a great way to look at the whole 'customer service,'..er .. I mean 'customer helping' situation. And even better yet, wouldn't it be great if we could get our employees to think of it this way too.

— Chapter 16 Notes —

PUNCH-OUT THOUGHTS:
- *So what's your job, what's your purpose? How would you define it in two or three sentences?*

- *Is your employees' job and purpose the same or is it different from yours? Why or Why Not?*

- *But even more important, what kinds of things can be done to begin the education process so all of your people understand their purpose and the value they bring to their company and themselves? What kind of ideas can you come up with?*

- *Who would have to be involved to start this process? Are their people outside your immediate store that should be involved? Are there things you could do to help this all begin?*

EPILOGUE

Based on years of retail experience, I decided to end this book with my top ten list of "Rules For Retailers To Live By." I figured, almost everyone has a top ten list so why not me? But developing the list turned out to be much harder than I expected ... I could only come up with seven rules. Obviously, you can't have a top ten list with only seven items ... so here's what I'm doing.

First, sit back, relax and read my seven rules ... I think they're great. Then, after you've finished, take a minute or two and put together a few of your own you think I should include to finish out my list. Then send them to me and let's see if I select one of yours to finish out my Top Ten. Enjoy my top seven list.

#7 Retailer Rule To Live By
Since it's the early worm that gets eaten by the early bird, ... sleep late.

This is absolutely great advice ... if you're a worm. I guess it just comes down to what you want to be ... scrounge around on the ground like a worm, or fly high and soar like a bird. If it's the worm, then stay in bed and let someone else dictate how you will live ... but if it's the bird, you've got to get out and get going, take chances, learn to fly, and go after the things you want. Bird or worm? It's really your choice!

#6 Retailer Rule To Live By
Stay patient and understand some days you're the pigeon, and others you're the statue!

Some days it just seems everything goes wrong: deliveries don't show up on time; employees call in sick; displays get knocked over; someone hits a pole and the power goes out; etc. But don't let it get you upset. Instead, just think of it as this is your day to be the statue ... tomorrow you'll probably be the pigeon and then you can really fly.

#5 Retailer Rule To Live By
Leave your ego at the door and remember, you're only as good as your last inventory.

In retail, we're only as good as our last inventory. That's the way it is! That's the way it works! Shrink, gross profit and net profit calculations are all based on an accurate inventory count so no matter how many good periods we've had, it's the last one everyone remembers. So try to stay balanced with the good ones, and fight to keep from jumping off the nearest cliff when a less than good one shows up.

#4 Retailer Rule To Live By
Stay positive, even though at times you may feel your sole purpose in life is to serve as a warning to others.

I once had a friend tell me, *"Things are never as good or as bad as they may appear at the time."* I have found this to be absolutely true. It's always amazed me how different my perspective can be in 24 hours. So, stay positive, don't give up, and keep moving forward.

#3 Retailer Rule To Live By
Always keep your words soft and sweet, just in case you have to eat them.

No matter what you think about a particular person, always assume you're going to meet them again. You'll be amazed how many times this really does happen. So keep your words soft and sweet and NEVER, EVER, burn bridges.

If you get mad and want to send an email or note ... write the piece, save it, go home and get a good night's rest. Next day open it up, reread it, smile and then throw the whole dumb thing away. This one little trick will save you more embarrassment and heartache than you can ever imagine. Believe me, I know firsthand, but that's another story!

#2 Retailer Rule To Live By
Never put both feet in your mouth at the same time, ... you won't have a leg to stand on.

Have you ever had a situation where you became so focused on proving a point that you forgot why the point was important in the first place? Be careful here, keep your emotions in check and try to keep at least one foot out of your mouth at all times.

Yeah, I know that isn't always possible, but be careful when you're running your mouth before you put your brain in gear.

#1 Retailer Rule To Live By

Don't get upset, but remember, 20 'Atta Boys' can be wiped out by just 1 'Ah Sh_t.'

In retail it seems to make little difference how many good things we've done ... how many sales or profit records we've broken or how many months of good gross profits we've had ... all it takes is one "Ah Sh_t" moment, and the slate gets wiped clean and we start back at zero. And maybe that's the way it should be. Retail is about <u>today</u>, about <u>this moment</u>, about the customers we work with <u>right now</u>.

Oh yes, we might have a good relationship with a particular customer. They may like us and we might like them and things may have been good in the past. But that customer still wants to know, "How are you going to help me solve **today's** problem?" and "What can you do for me, **today**?" That's what retail is all about ... today, right now!

QUOTES

I've always been fascinated by quotes from other people on topics I'm particularly interested in. It amazes me how others may have the same thoughts or ideas as myself, but then are able to present them in such an elegant and enduring fashion. I've used a good number of quotes in the book, and here's some information about their originators.

Steven Covey (1932 - 2012) American educator, author, businessman and keynote speaker who wrote *The Seven Habits of Highly Successful People*

Benjamin Disraeli (1804 - 1881) British conservative politician, writer and aristocrat who twice served as Prime Minister

Jodie Foster (1962 -) — American actress, film director, producer, who speaks three languages and graduated 'magna cum laude' from Yale.

Robert Gately, President & CEO, Campbell Farming Corporation

Jeffrey Gitomer (1946 -) American author, professional speaker and business trainer who writes and lectures internationally on customer loyalty and personal development

Ray Kroc (1902 - 1984) American businessman who joined McDonald's in 1954 and built it into the most successful fast food operation in the world

Abraham Lincoln (1809 - 1865) American lawyer, statesman and 16th president of the United States

Vince Lombardi (1913 - 1970) American football player, coach and executive best known as the head coach of the Green Bay Packers during the 1960's

Og Mandino (1923 - 1996) American author of "*The Greatest Salesman In The World*," and past president of *Success Unlimited* Magazine

Stanley J. Randall (1908 - 1989) Ontario businessman and political figure who served as V.P. of the Canadian Manufacturers Association and chairman of the Ontario Economic Council

ABOUT THE AUTHOR

• Speaker • Author • Writer • Consultant • Educator

Buck is an industry-renowned food executive with a multifaceted background encompassing sales, marketing, operations and business development. He began his career while in high school and 18 years later, held a corporate Vice President position for one of the largest supermarket companies in the country.

He formed his own company in the 90's and has:
- worked with both domestic and foreign retailers and manufacturers in improving their business
- been a featured key-note speaker on numerous national platforms
- developed and managed the D.A.T.E.™ training program used nationally by the supermarket industry, reaching more than 16,000 supermarkets nationwide annually
- wrote and published his own industry training newsletter for twelve years reaching more than 1,000 retail and manufacturing companies
- wrote industry column and section for the supermarket's national trade publication for 6 years
- has been very heavily involved in the development of training and educational concepts for the supermarket industry.

This is his first book but a second, due for release in the summer of 2015, is already in the works.

Follow Buck on ...
- Facebook at — www.facebook.com/mybucksworth
- Twitter at — A Bucks Worth

Don't Forget Your Free Gift

Many of the topics in this book are covered in our "Think About It" Video series. Included with this book is a free copy of ...

NOW I'M A MANAGER, WHAT THINGS SHOULD I DO DIFFERENTLY?

... which discusses the information presented in the first chapter of this book.

Just go to:
www.abucksworth.com/lead-page-43264
and download your Free Video

Some of the other topics covered in our "Think About It" series include ...
- The Difference Between Good and Great Customer Service
- Setting Ourselves Up To Succeed, Not Fail
- How To Know We've Given Good Service
- How To Deal With Difficult Customers
- Great Salesmen Don't Just Tell or Show, They Demonstrate
- People Quit Their Boss Before They Quit Their Company
- A Leader's Most Important Job is To Mentor
- Motivation, Is Necessity Because Not Everyone Is As Good As You
- Getting 'C's' To Produce As 'A's'
- Recognition: The Key To Higher Performance
- How To Find The Best People
- Making Decisions Based On Customer Needs
- Be A Salesperson, Not An Order Taker
- You Get What You Inspect, Not Expect

A Buck's Worth

... and many others!
A Buck's Worth • 190 E Stacy #306-273 Allen, Tx 75002 • (214) 383-3442